THE

ASK

FRAMEWORK

Carole Stizza

PCC, SHRM-SCP

THE

ASK

FRAMEWORK

REDEMPTION
PRESS

Published by Redemption Press, PO Box 427, Enumclaw, WA 98022.

Toll-Free (844) 2REDEEM (273-3336)

Redemption Press is honored to present this title in partnership with the author. The views expressed or implied in this work are those of the author. Redemption Press provides our imprint seal representing design excellence, creative content, and high quality production.

ISBN 13: 978-1-68314-838-8 (Paperback)
978-1-68314-839-5 (ePub)
978-1-68314-840-1 (Mobi)

Library of Congress Catalog Card Number: 2020923540

Choose with Care.
Why?
Choice pulls from either Faith or Fear.
Where there is Fear there is no Faith,
And where there is Faith, there is no Fear.
Choose wisely.

~Anonymous

Author's Note

We all grow up and have different experiences to lead the lives we have. Along the way, certain words and phrases have become guiding touchstones. Quotes sprinkled throughout this book have each meant something to me at a certain time in my life—some are spiritual, and some are inspirational. I encourage you to collect the touchstones that remind you of your journey to greatness and to value yourself and those around you too. One of my favorite quotes by Jack Canfield is, "Everything you want is on the other side of fear."[1]

There have been many times while writing this book that I stopped, pressed the Pause button, redirected the content and purpose, and wished for an easier, less scary path in conveying my thoughts. Many times I reminded myself that frustration is a daily friend—it's how we respond to it that makes the differences in what we achieve.

When you find the quotes that help you live a braver life, do not judge where they come from. How you use them determines your path of greatness.

Contents

Introduction

This Book Started Because . . .

I sat, frustrated, gripping the steering wheel while still sitting in the parking garage before heading home. White knuckled and internally yelling at myself, I couldn't believe I had found myself on the receiving end of a lunch with two bosses who fumbled their way through what was supposed to be a performance review!

Twelve months of suffering in a role that left me unchallenged, unmotivated, and unfulfilled—and now with no information of where to grow in the organization—I felt lost. We've all had a bad day. We've seen the scene in a movie that caused the character to grow, change, or see the world differently. For me this was one of those days that started a chain reaction to now.

A simple performance review that finally revealed what I had suspected all along—I was working for a person in a role above their experience, and I was paying for it on the short end of the underappreciated, underpaid, and overlooked stick! Prior to this, I had never been reviewed as anything less than a rock star in my abilities as a professional. What had gone so wrong?

Sitting at an awkward lunch, the founder of the company and my immediate boss were sitting across from me. These were people I had trusted to step up to recognize my contributions. Instead of talking about the significant work I had accomplished, the projects I had started and completed, what I had added to the organization, and how well I'd done, my boss joked and made fun of my small discrepancies, grammatical errors, and insignificant mistakes in my work—leaving me feeling picked on and belittled. I sat there dumbstruck.

At no time did either my immediate boss or her boss take my performance review seriously. What was going on? Anytime there was a pause, as if to say, *OK, let's get to the real reason we are here*, the joking started all over again, as if on repeat by default. I was rendered speechless.

Did my boss really know what to do in a performance review? Especially in front of *the* boss? Making a joke about my mistakes seemed to be the only point. Would this ever end? Wouldn't either of them take the initiative to ask about my contributions? My brain seemed paralyzed to intervene.

Then my gut started to talk—as loud as a banging drum. The overwhelming screaming from my gut said, *QUIT NOW! Politely put in your two weeks' notice and turn this into an exit interview. NOW! Get the right attention of how badly this all went and MOVE ON!*

Move on? Without a job to go to?

The angel and devil were at war, sitting on either side of my head, begging me to act.

Instead I sat frozen at that lunch, as if watching a horror show. And now, in my car, I sat fuming! And then it slowly dawned on me—I wasn't fuming because of the performance review. I was fuming because I was so mad at myself for having sat there, a mute and silent witness to such a bad showcase of management. Even worse, I had settled for such a crappy job, and deep down I had known this was a poor job fit from the beginning. Almost as soon as I started working there.

Yes, I'd landed the job during an economic downturn. Yes, jobs were hard to find because so many other people were looking while companies were trying to work with a leaner workforce. Settling for a job I knew was wrong the first week into it had stolen my ability to see straight and to think critically about what I could be doing, and now it seemed to have also stolen my confidence.

The job I'd thought I had agreed to was a management role. Instead the job duties quickly became those of being the personal assistant to the new office manager, a prior project accountant who had talked their way into an empty slot. I was asked for my expertise in what to do as a manager and then watched as decisions were made from an accounting perspective. Ugh! Why had I not left immediately upon realizing the job advertisement had been a ruse?

That was when a bigger realization hit me—*hard*!

I sank into my seat. I still hadn't turned the key to drive home.

The realization was that when the jobs became scarce, the economy in a recession, I had forgotten to trust my instincts. Forgotten what made me successful in other roles. And what was most unsettling, I couldn't remember how that loss of myself had started. All I knew now was that I needed to understand my value enough to determine what my unique gifts and talents meant to any organization, let alone this one.

That one day changed everything for me.

Within five years I not only had figured out how to solve my own value dilemma, I had stepped out of settling for jobs that limited my growth and into my own coaching practice, speaking internationally and conducting corporate workshops to elevate how people communicate, step into personal performance, and invite team engagement.

Looking back at that lunch, I remember hoping to be told about what I'd added to the organization, where I had added value, and what had gone right because of my addition to the team. With the economy still healing, growth for our office was imminent, as new clients were gained. I envisioned growth for my position as well.

In previous employment, I'd already experienced customized roles specifically carved out for me to grow in responsibilities. On this day I was eager to carve out a position that allowed me to take on different duties.

Now, as I look back on that exchange during my performance-review lunch, I can see that my boss must have been thinking the same thing. With both of us hungry for growth, the tactic to pick me apart positioned her far better than me at that moment. This is where my ability to step into the conversation and direct it with more positive outcomes for myself would have been ideal. Yet I was so surprised and taken aback at the joking—I froze.

I froze because I hadn't been prepared to defend myself or known that I would need to. To have the founder, who knew my work, be complicit by not stopping the attack might have been the bigger shock.

Sadly, many employees find themselves in similar positions—marginalized at the expense of someone else's ambition. Unless you have a clear picture of how well you perform, can clearly identify where your talent has been of value, and how it is perceived positively by others, you may feel as unprepared to defend yourself as I did that day—lost in an unfulfilling job, with a less-than-thrilling boss, in a flat hierarchal company.

For those in organizations with upper management, employees often wait for the opportunities to come to them—like within a feedback session or a performance review—trusting the reviewer to identify their value and offer their growth. When the opposite occurs, this leaves them unprepared to advocate for themselves, leaving little control in gaining any information desired. This is often why many dread review sessions—the lack of control of what information is received.

Research confirms that gaining performance feedback remains in the top five most undesirable experiences at work.[2] Either because the employee doesn't feel as if the work being reviewed is relevant, that the reviewer is biased and plays favorites to others, or that the review lens is based solely on the most recent work results (technically referenced as *recency bias*). When the employee in question (such as myself that day) isn't prepared to offer positive information to add and balance out any surprise negatives, the conclusion may lead to feeling as if the reviewer has set their mind about an employee's value. The result is a feeling of defeat.

As I drove home, I took stock. It was clear to me that I either didn't know my value or had forgotten my value and had definitely forgotten how to vouch for myself when I needed to.

The reasons I had considered taking the job, knowing the title was lesser than my previous one and simply wanting to get my foot in the door for more opportunity, seemed insignificant to what I was now losing—my confidence.

I'd relocated to the area, having made yet another military move. I had just left a sales director position and was looking for a new job, preferably where I could build upon my leadership and management experience and not just in sales.

The only reason I'd thought this job was a viable option was because I had risen in roles before. I'd applied as if this was a starting point to getting my foot in the door. It went south so fast, and I should have acted. Now I looked back and questioned why I stayed.

Was it the recent move?

Was it because I hadn't received a ton of interview requests due to the lagging economy?

Why had I questioned my value enough to stay in such a lesser position?

Did the economy really do that much damage to my critical thinking on opportunities?

Or had I settled, as if waiting for the economy to bounce back with more options magically appearing?

I can't go back in time to select which one mattered more. Ironically, I meet people who still question their value and settle for lesser roles now. With all the experts, psychologists, and self-help companies designed to help people step into their greatness, why do so many people still settle?

Since that day I've learned that most of us are functioning off limited information, limited ways to get the right information, and outdated habits that keep us there.

> Most of us are functioning off limited information, limited ways to get the right information, and outdated habits that keep us playing small.

Helping clients today overcome this challenge has come from an alarmingly simple insight that began with me suffering through that performance-review lunch. Whether the goal is to increase confidence, obtain the new promotion, or step into your leadership role with genuine excitement instead of fear, clients find what I'm offering in this book applicable, insightful, and a springboard for success.

This book is going to explain a simple framework to use and apply to find the very information that will help you celebrate who you are, what gifts you offer others, and how to step into being your best self—your own Super Powerful Best self—while you look for exciting ways to grow.

Many employees, and even entrepreneurs and executives, think they know their value due to the results placed on their résumé. Yes, this all helps. Yet if asked to talk about themselves in an interview in reference to their specific talents, they tend to offer only what they did right to get specific results—not what they naturally do well all the time. What Tania Katan, author and speaker, calls your Superhero Powers.[3]

We hear this in interviews when someone stumbles on the strength and weakness questions, resorting to offering what they did in the last project that helped other people succeed. This leaves the interpretation of their strengths up to the interviewer to interpret their true abilities, forfeiting control of what the interviewer needs to hear.

To be clear, few of us spend the right amount of time reveling in what we do well enough to understand how relevant it is to our value at work. We don't collect insights into how others perceive our success, our talents, or our strengths. Few employees get up every day reminding themselves of what they do well or the positive traits others have identified as their contributions at work, or spend any time celebrating what they don't have to change in order to succeed at work.

Making this even harder to embrace today is the new need to work more virtually. Now, the biggest concern elevating feelings of insecurity is feeling invisible.[4] We know this because as I write this, we are in the pandemic of 2020, in a mask-debatable, hand-washing alert, shelter-in-place mandated nonessential personnel quarantine. We are all working from home more than in any time in history to try and keep hospitals from being overwhelmed with newly infected people.

The economy has suffered greatly, and employees who still have a job are working virtually. Those who do not have a job are now pondering how to determine the job market under a quarantine. Whether having a job, or jobless, all are grappling with feeling invisible right now. And now is the most important time for everyone to be reminded of what they do right, what they need to honor about themselves to obtain success, and how to communicate their value.

When I finally turned the ignition key and started driving home after my performance review, I came to a new realization about my own sense of value. I realized I had felt unprepared to defend my value to the projects and accomplishments I'd achieved because I wasn't prepared to verbalize my specific value as a professional who offered unique strengths and assets to *any* company.

I didn't have the words because I didn't know what I did uniquely well compared to others. Not in the sense of right and wrong, but rather the things I did well because of who I was as a whole person. If I was struggling with this, having had a successful career before this day, I knew I wasn't alone.

I'd heard this same complaint from others and thought I knew what they meant—until I was in the very position to stand up for my skills and talents and didn't have the words. The mental stumble came from a lack of practice in knowing what to say, how to say it, and why it was needed.

I realized then that when any of us get asked questions such as "What are your strengths?" "What value would your employment mean to the organization?" and "What assets do you bring to the team?" we guess as to what the person asking wants or needs to hear.

We stop thinking about offering them what we know about ourselves, and even if we did have the words, we don't offer examples to support the information we offer. Both are a powerful combo, yet we don't practice offering this information.

Why? Because we don't typically think this way—ever! Thus, we stumble collectively. And when this happens, our confidence takes the hit, fast and hard. We start looking for solutions.

Picture this: Someone walks by selling a simple box. You're not buying any old box—not interested. But then you read the sign around the seller's neck, *Need Confidence?* and you *run* to buy that box, hoping the secret to your confidence is in there. Why? Because we go after anything that helps us deal with our most painful problem. We go for the painkiller as fast as possible.

During that lunch, I would have eagerly bought that box had it been available that day. Instead I felt lost and alone. My disappearing confidence was my problem. Without my confidence, I had forgotten my own superhero qualities and the words needed to redirect that lunch conversation. I needed to find a solution for this *fast*.

For me, finding solutions like this drives me to look at new research.

Research has given me solutions before, and now I was looking again—with laser focus!

What I found was new research that took me by surprise. I didn't believe it would work.

Until I tried putting it to work. It was awkward at first. Anything new is hard to try if you haven't seen someone else do it. It takes some guts to do anything new. My need pushed me past the awkwardness and fear and helped me chose faith instead. Faith to try at least. And it worked beautifully!

I imagine others will resist too, just like me, until they realize the solution is easier than they first think.

I had one client tell me that they didn't think they wanted to learn what others felt they did right, or what other people felt they didn't need to change, because they preferred to question their confidence to give them the edge they needed to have more relatable empathy with others. As if feeling less-than makes one more relatable! Expressing empathy or being relatable has extraordinarily little to do with a lack of confidence—let's be clear.

Once I was able to unpack this new framework with the client, they found that their gift *is* empathy and relatability, not a lack of confidence. Talk about a new perspective!

I had another client point blank tell me they were scared to concentrate on what they did right or what made them unique, because they didn't want to get too cocky. As if knowledge alone would change their attitude or the way they acted at work.

Do we falsely think that knowing what we do right, what makes us special and unique, would suddenly deny us the humility we find valuable? If so, we are wrong! We all need to find out what makes us unique, how we are divinely made, and what helps us stand out in the crowd from others.

Without this information, you may find yourself at an awkward lunch, being marginalized by someone else's ambition, too stunned and ill prepared to boldly step into offering what makes the organization better because you are there. Like I did.

When I set out to solve this problem for myself, I found ways to go after positive information when I needed it, step off the hamster wheel of perpetual self-improvement, quiet the loud voices of not being enough in my head, and step into where my true genius could be realized.

I found how my gifts show up at work and have helped me prosper in the growth of my business, the depth of professional relationships, and in connecting with my friends and family. I'm not perfect—by no means. Being human is a constant state of growth, which is exactly why sharing this has been the greatest gift.

When I help others to embrace the concept in this book, the best news is their confidence returns, the proof of their gifts starts becoming more visible to them, the ideas of promotions and doing more challenging work suddenly take shape again, and the ability to go after the right information about themselves is born.

Over the next fifteen chapters, I will share with you this concept of how you can step into conversations that hold true gems of information about what you do that you could honor and what you can nurture for change that comes from growth. Nurturing change is an integral component of personal and professional growth. We all like to grow.

In contrast, we don't like to change when change is pushed upon us. So before you blindly accept that change is needed or go after changing anything, take a moment and pause, take a deep breath, and rethink. Knowing what makes you unique allows you to know what *not* to change.

In this book we will explore why this approach is needed now more than ever and how it flies in the face of the self-improvement industry. Once you learn more about this approach, you'll be eager to implement it to focus your professional growth.

When introducing the framework within this approach, we'll walk through the challenge of deciding when to move forward, and I'll show you why the efforts of changing your view on gaining information this way will pay off. We will walk through each step of the framework with examples, and I'll show you how to take this approach with you into the workplace to elevate professional relationships and team engagement results.

Research and data are provided, as well as the speed bumps found when trying to adopt anything new—such as this approach.

And tips to avoid toxic results, both at work and at home, are offered with examples. There are gifts to be discovered, and I cannot wait to help you find them!

There will be many times in your life where you will be asked to communicate your value and how others succeed by working with you. There will be times when you will need to step up and communicate your value to offset someone's misplaced ambitions or a boss's lack of perspective or to gain the right role.

While your family will love you at the end of every day, there will be a chapter dedicated to sharing this with them too. I will end by challenging you to teach this same approach to others, and I can't wait to share with you how to do that while you elevate your relationships too.

To start, let's grab what you need to go after (to gain) the right information, regain your confidence, and elevate your knowledge of you at your best for the professional growth you love.

The bonus: by using the framework offered in this book, you will also be able to connect with the very people who love you and may feel they know you best. Learning how they see you may blow your socks off, and it is the best information to go after when looking to understand the best about yourself.

There will be some inner noise to cut through as you move forward with this work. When you follow this approach, you will transform the way you think about the type of information you share and how you communicate your value in any given situation. This will transform the way you step forward in your life—both personally and professionally.

> If the pain points people experience result in the first question being, "What do I need to change for my life to get better?" You are asking the wrong question.

The Confidence Gap

While driving home, I recalled all the past jobs I had wanted and not applied for after not getting the first couple of jobs from interviews. I saw a recurring theme in my approach. I realized how my lack of ability to communicate my value had contributed to my current pain. With my head shaking side to side, I spoke to myself in the rearview mirror: "Carole, you've never answered the most important questions!"

My mind wandered back to the following memories. When asked, "Can you share an example of how you perform at work?" "Can you clearly identify where your talent has been of value?" "Do you know how you are perceived positively by others?" I would simply list the successes I had achieved, note the rewards accepted, or recite performance-review results. This is what I came to learn is simply providing side information or no information at all. In truth, I wasn't prepared to answer them correctly.

Looking back and culminating all my time in human resources interviewing others for job openings, I can now decipher how I, and many others, were making the same mistake. The following questions are only examples, but these questions are at the crux of your self-awareness and knowledge of how well you can communicate your performance and your influence.

The Three Questions

1. "Can you share an example of how well you perform at work?"

When asked, I would fumble around in my head. You know that feeling. You're literally reaching through cobwebs up there to recall any facts you've been given from compliments, prior performance reviews, or praise from a client. You are searching for other people's words.

I would come up with an example of a project I worked on and explain the details, as if the interviewer would pull out of that what I did well. When I was still met with wanting expressions from the interviewer, they would ask follow-up questions to pull it out of me.

What they really needed to hear was my understanding of which skills and talents I specifically offered and how that experience allowed me to bring more skills and talents to the new role.

Basically, I wasn't answering the question. Even when I would regurgitate any compliments, reviews, and praise, I wasn't speaking in first person—I was offering words of other people.

How did I know how well I performed at work? I know I worked hard and delivered results. I knew I got praise. I knew I helped the clients get the results they wanted, but I didn't know specifics. And specifics are what helps our confidence hold on to the positives about ourselves. Without specifics, it's hard to hear the great things we do. And specifics are individual.

Take Sean.

Sean sat dejected. He came and slumped down on the chair facing my desk. The desk I used when I was on site, hired as the HR consultant. He had just finished a meeting regarding his performance, which was solid. I didn't understand his mood.

"Sean, what gives? You seem confused by the results you received. What questions do you have?"

"I don't get it. I've been busting my butt, and I can't figure out why I keep getting a rating of four out of five when I know I'm worthy of top ratings. And"—he paused—"I was hoping for a raise."

"Sean, what questions did you ask to find out how to get up to the rating of the five you want?"

After several moments replied, "After I looked at the ratings on the report they handed me, I think I froze. My mind just started to go back over all I do and what they expected. I just couldn't comprehend what wasn't good enough to get the highest marks. I mean, I feel like I kill myself and go above and beyond all the time. What are they expecting for me to move the needle from a four to a five if I'm not already doing it?"

I asked again if he had thought to ask them about this during the review, and he shook his head. "I actually thought they would tell me, but all they did was tell me how well my work was received and how much they appreciated me."

I looked at him. "Do you remember what they said about what you do well and what they appreciate about you?"

He shrugged. "Seemed to be the same stuff that I know I do well—but now I don't believe them, because it doesn't seem to be good enough to get the highest marks, so I don't even know why to keep trying or what to do better. With the four rating, I didn't even bother to ask for a raise. I'm not sure what to do."

I recognized Sean's plight.

He had become deaf to what he did well. He wanted to know how to be the best at what he did, and the gap between the ratings he received and what was said didn't line up. At least not enough for him to be inspired to hear them. He was discouraged, and when this happens, great talent like Sean start to look elsewhere for growth and success.

Now let's contrast this with another type of experience. Meet John.

Early in his military career, John walked in for his performance review with his boss. A prepared stay-on-top-of-it kind of guy, John was proactive, aware, and looking for growth. The military has a formal progression system of promotion, yet if one is not careful, time can run out to obtain all the steps required to be ready for advancement. Not John. He was methodical, careful, and open and eager to learn how to move forward with leadership skills. He had also been to many other performance reviews and was anticipating more of the same. He received a surprise! His boss had taken the typical 0 to 10 rating scale used for performance reviews, marked out the 0, and put in a 9.

Recognizing John's surprise, his boss offered, "John, you are already doing everything to a hard nine of excellence, so I wanted to use this time to identify the small nuances we can implement for you to get from a nine to a ten every time, every day, and with every person you lead."

John was so impressed with how helpful this method of review was that he put the same technique into practice for every performance review he gave to those on his own team.

From that day forward, John marked out the 0 to establish the excellence baseline and work on tweaking the right things. Like John, who came out of that review able to appreciate what he already was doing well *and* have new information to use, the people he led from that day forward were rewarded with the same experience.

Unlike Sean, John was given specific information verbally. Where Sean's confidence took a hit, John's was elevated. John didn't need to implement the approach and formula I'm offering in this book—he was provided the information he needed and could use it so well that he was able to do the same for others.

In contrast, Sean's situation highlights what can happen when one is not prepared to ask for the information needed. Sean felt personally shunned when he saw his ratings. He resigned shortly after his performance review to work with a competitor, still unprepared to step into the conversations around performance. After Sean's departure, I was able to sit down and discuss aspects of the performance review with his supervisor. (Confidentiality of Sean's conversation prevented me from being direct with his manager at the time, yet I urged them to have a deeper conversation on what Sean's performance added to the team. I may never know if that conversation happened, but upon Sean's departure, I did sit down and discuss aspects of the performance review that potentially led to this outcome.)

The supervisor had been surprised at Sean's departure yet respected his desire to move on to new challenges. He never realized that Sean's departure had been provoked due to the performance review or that the lack of information about rating numbers would have such a profound effect on someone as high performing as Sean. And yes, Sean's boss was one of those leaders who believed that if you gave anyone the top mark on any aspect of their job, they would become complacent and unmotivated.

I was able to explain that most employees, once they've hit the top mark, are expecting the goal post to move—meaning that the next top mark to hit presents more challenge. This provides a win-win for both employee and supervisor. He hadn't ever looked at it that way.

If Sean had been prepared to answer any of the questions in this chapter, before his review, he might have been able to ask better questions to identify if the employer felt the same way. Without the specifics he was looking for to support his idea of his success, his shaken confidence made him feel as if he needed to move on.

I imagine this happens often to many of us. At least I hear about it often. When the desire exists to help people communicate their value, clarifying the specifics that resonate with them matters.

2. "Can you clearly identify where your talent has been of value?"

I dreaded this question. Mainly because it would stump me when asked. OK, not entirely. I knew which projects my efforts and skills had helped produce great results for, and I could answer that part of the question. But if a follow-up question pushed me to express the value of my talent, I was at a loss. Even the most benign question like "Which skill do you feel was valued the most in the project?" left me fumbling for an answer. I was still dependent upon words other people had offered.

Like the first question's dilemma, I was still dependent upon whatever praise was still floating around in my head. I hadn't intentionally paid attention to how other people *valued* my talent—at least not enough to recognize it as that. I also didn't know how to ask for that type of information. I would defer back to thinking about what I had been paid and why. That's not useful. Why? Because your value is not always the price tag.

Your Value = Your Superhero Powers

What are Superhero Powers? If you considered all the superheroes, like the ones we've read about in comic strips, seen in movies and shows, or portrayed in real life, Superhero Powers are used to help others. The opposite of superheroes are villains who use their powers to hurt others.

Since we are not functioning out of a comic strip or movie, we get to rely on our natural strengths. What you do naturally is considered a natural strength, fueled by how you think, what motivates you, and where you get your energy in all you do. Your strengths show up at work. When they are used to help others, you get credited for the value they bring to the team. That value becomes what you are known for—these become your Superhero Powers.

For the record, the value that you and others regard as deserved, important, and useful can be anything you do that is valued by others. This value is often monetized within a work setting—a raise, a promotion, a bonus can often follow a job well done that helps the organization win new business or brilliantly succeed in any way. Yet how you know they value your talent isn't always in the price tag. I say this because of the ongoing inequality of pay between genders, industries, and perceptions of supply and demand. Don't estimate your value solely on what you've been paid or offered. It's a false foundation.

So how do you find out this novel value superhero quality information? That's what I wanted to know too!

So did Claire.

Claire was up for a promotion and felt that she had answered the promotion board's questions with clarity. She had been nervous, yes, but felt she had shared how she guided projects successfully to the finish line, and she'd recited the compliments received about exceeding client expectations. She offered how she had developed her team and the expectations she had placed on them that were met.

Claire didn't receive the promotion.

When she was passed over for the promotion, she received insights from her mentor. The mentor, equally frustrated with her not getting the promotion, offered that the board felt she hadn't been able to give them a good sense of her value and confidence as a leader. Clair was baffled. She pushed for more specifics. What she learned perplexed her.

The board had expected to hear what she could offer about what her team would say about her, her leadership, and what she felt were her shining qualities as their leader. Basically, what would her team brag about regarding her leadership? Or how would she brag about her leadership?

She fumed. And then paused. How was she supposed to offer this information when she didn't have this information? How was she supposed to gain this information? Asking her team seemed so egotistical. She was stumped, confused, and disappointed. That's when we started to work together.

If you are thinking that there were other ways for the board to gain this information from her employees, there were. That wasn't the point. They were expecting her, as a leader, to be more confident in what she offered as a leader and to gain this information from her team too, as a way of staying connected to her team and being ready to take on the additional leadership requirements being offered. This highlights an aspect of our work relationships we are not used to considering.

What do people brag about when asked, "What it's like to work with us?"

That's a big question. And it's one that we can't entirely answer ourselves without input from others. Yes, we can brag, but it's from our own perspective, which stems from our own inner ego. And our ego is normally aspirational in who we *want* to be.

It's not like we go about our day bragging about each other either. No, we are normally in problem-solving mode and focused entirely on how to solve things—not *who* solved it.

The answer to the question "What is it like to work with you?" ultimately stems from needing to figure out how to answer the last question:

3. "Do you know how you are perceived positively by others?"

There is an important aspect to this question—the use of the word *positively*. And this stumps us all. Why? Because we don't know how to ask for it. And when we do ask for information about our performance, or any aspect of our work, we aren't specific enough.

Sean was so discouraged during his review that he froze up and never asked anything. John was provided such specific information that he never thought to ask for additional information. And then there was Claire being told what they needed her to offer, and lastly, me on that frustrating day when I didn't know which questions to ask to drive the review conversation into anything meaningful.

When we aren't prepared with what to ask or how to ask for it, we fall into the trap of letting other people tell us everything. I call this the "What do you think?" trap.

Chapter 1 Questions

1. What is exciting about learning your Superhero Powers?
2. If you knew your own unique superpowers, how would that shift your professional and personal experiences?

The "What Do You Think?" Trap

What would happen if no one wanted you to change—ever! Would that free you from feeling judged, criticized, or evaluated? This idea is such a weird one that most people look at me funny, then smile, then breathe deep . . . and then admit how cool that would be. It doesn't mean you won't want to change in a growing way—it just means you get to be in control of what you change and when you do it. How refreshing! This book is designed to help you embrace how you don't have to change—by how you go about asking questions about what others already like and love about you. You get to discover the things you do so well that others want them to remain. This is looking for the positive before you introduce change.

When given this task, my first reaction is to gravitate toward things my family doesn't want to see change, like foods I cook that they love. These foods are often the center of well-loved traditions. I've come to realize that the importance of tradition is the feeling of belonging in a safe place. So when I tried a new recipe on my mashed potatoes at Thanksgiving one year, I quickly learned how much my daughter loved the old recipe more.

When people are part of a tradition, there is normally an aspect of the tradition they like most. They become more emotionally attached than they realize—either through smell, taste, or memory.[5] My daughter had no idea how much she liked those mashed potatoes until she realized how much she had been looking forward to them—and when I had changed them, she was surprised at her disappointment. Many family fights often begin when one part of a tradition gets changed without consideration of those who liked that part more than the others. We howl with laughter when we see it on a sitcom; in real life it's more painful. I now know how my daughter prefers her mashed potatoes and smile at the lesson.

I use the food example simply to bring about the point of asking. One of our former traditions was providing each person's favorite foods when they arrived home from college or a long trip. For health reasons, I've begun eliminating animal products and have adapted recipes. I'm comfortable asking what family and friends think of new variations because I know we are all judging the present foods based on prior great experiences of the same recipe. I'm curious when I've changed any ingredient.

When we learn what people like, we often are presenting a product or experience in which we easily ask, "So what do you think?" We are often met with words of appreciation and specifics about what they like the most, because when it comes to food, my family has a relationship established on trust and shared experiences. And we ask this question with certain expectations.

When it's not food, we also have a familiarity with each other that includes trust, in most cases. However, there are other, newer territories that emerge where feelings can still get hurt when asked, "What do you think?"—and then met with an unexpected answer.

This question becomes even more dynamic at work. Work presents unique situations, especially when we are offering small portions of work as part of a larger project, or a team, or in segments doled out on a timeline to a customer. How do you know what people think of your work then? You *do* have to ask if you want to know the answer. Waiting around for others to compliment you or give you specifics isn't a healthy way to assess your work.

But do you really want to ask, "What do you think?" I shied away from this question often because I couldn't guarantee I would get positive information, and most days I wasn't shopping for a negative comment. So this question doesn't get presented in the right way. Why? Because by itself, this question can open you up for a lot more information than you sometimes want.

I know—I have some ego-bruising experiences with this. I fell into the "What do you think?" trap when I was working on a customer service campaign as part of a team with a virtual company. Here's what happened: We each had specific work to submit for review and had agreed on a timeline that would allow time for the report to be cohesively formatted. I even turned in my section of work a day early! I wanted to provide more space for review. At the time I was dreadfully sick with a sinus infection and had gone over the piece repeatedly, making sure I hadn't missed anything. I felt good about the content, as I had double-checked the details, though I'd paid little attention to formatting. I was relying on our team member to take care of the formatting.

I asked, "What do you think?" when I emailed my section in.

We've all asked similar questions. We've all sent a quick email with a short hello and a one-liner: "Thoughts?" is one. "Looking for feedback" is another.

The most common mistake in asking this question is in expecting to get the news we want to hear. What I received was not exactly what I had hoped for. I did receive positive information on the content—that was my specialty. I got ripped to shreds on the formatting, font, and punctuation—not my specialty. I was confused as to why this type of feedback was coming my way. When I asked about the formatting feedback, I quickly learned that the formatter was also sick and that everyone was doing their best to do their own formatting. Indignant, I wanted to retort that I didn't know the formatter was sick, but it didn't really matter. I had to go back and do my own formatting, which isn't my strong suit, and do it while also sick. I was as grumpy as the person who had responded to my email. I learned then that when I want to ask for feedback, I needed to find a better way.

The first way I found was simply providing specific context, which I could have achieved by asking, "What do you think about the content at this point?" The message back may have not been so angry and may have also posed a request to do my own formatting under the circumstances—providing a completely different tone and less drama.

Context helps with clarity. Without it, you leave yourself wide open to get unexpected information.

I fell into the same trap as Thomas.

Thomas was a new engineer in a local firm. Hired during a company growth spurt, he quickly noticed that most of the engineers came from the same university—just not his. It seems that the founder preferred engineers who had training from his alma mater. Thomas simply had to learn how they connected. Thomas quickly fit in with the other engineers, and they socialized outside of work. However, not long after he was hired, I noticed he had become quieter at work than when he started. I didn't know if he was quieter because of workload, the need for concentration, looming deadlines, or something else. At the time I was supporting the growing administrative staff.

One day we were chatting, and he said something that caught my attention. "I don't think I fit in as well as I thought."

"What do you mean?" I asked.

"I just never get any positive feedback on my work."

"Is all your work returned for corrections?"

"No."

"Then what are you basing this feeling on?"

"Well, when I ask for feedback on my work, all I get is what is wrong. As if they are just looking for what needs to be better instead of what I'm doing right. I'm always asking what they think about my progress, or on what I'm turning in, and all I get is negatives."

"How are you asking for information?" I asked.

"I ask them, 'What do you think?'"

The open-ended "What do you think?" wreaks havoc. It opens a window for uncensored information to flow, with no framework for positives or negatives. No context. A single piece of negative information denies you the opportunity to celebrate anything you are doing right. It throws you off balance.

When I had the chance to talk to Thomas's boss, he was surprised to realize how Thomas was taking the information. Turns out, he'd thought that since Thomas was new, and he asked so often, he was asking for instruction. Thomas's boss wasn't spending any time reminding Thomas of what he was doing well. The supervisor was just trying to help Thomas get better as fast as possible. He genuinely thought Thomas was doing a lot well.

I reminded him this wasn't all on Thomas. The lack of context on what Thomas needed to hear could just as easily be remedied if he were asked for context too. As Thomas's boss, it was in his best interests to assess and remind Thomas of what was going right and where areas for growth existed.

A growing body of research is highlighting the benefits of using positive psychology and appreciative inquiry to exchange information by communicating positive information more than negative information. As more and more employees report a growing desire for recognition, exchanging positive information more than negative information may organically fit this need. Positive information is identified by employees as desired recognition.[6]

And recognition is the number one way to drive positive productivity. Bamboo HR recently reported that people will improve the thing they get recognition for so they can earn even more recognition. I was stunned to learn that 82 percent of employees find it annoying to not get recognized for what they accomplish or for their contributions to the team and organization, which, truth be told, I could relate to. More surprising, though, 49 percent will leave their job for a company that does recognize their employees.[7] Gone are the days when people would just "put their head down and tough it out." Which is great, because it is pushing leaders to recognize how to stay engaged with the needs of their organizations.

Perhaps that's why so many millennials wanted more feedback when they first entered the workforce.

> Whenever you are recognized and praised for any accomplishment by someone whose opinion you hold in high regard, your self-esteem goes up, along with your eagerness and enthusiasm to do even better on the job.
> —Brian Tracy

If you're wondering if Thomas is one of those millennials who needed a lot of feedback, yes, he is a millennial. Millennials have been credited for bringing more feedback front and center,[8] yet it is not just millennials who appreciate timely information on what they are doing. We all want to know we are on the right track when needing to produce good work. Millennials are just the most vocal and talk with their feet faster than any generation before them. We need to pay attention. In a survey done by Deloitte, it was stated that millennials will be 75 percent of our workforce in the year 2025.[9] However, in a more recent review of data, that number will most likely be 40 percent due to the continued working of older workers and other factors not used in the Deloitte survey.[10] Regardless if your team consists of millennials or other generational talent, all report that good feedback will help them lead faster and more effectively.

Currently, as reported by research within human resource forums, employees want some form of recognition every seven days, yet only 12 percent of employees say they receive appreciation for great work. Data helps us identify what types of recognition are more desirable:

- 30 percent want to be recognized with growth opportunities in the company;
- 28 percent just want praise;
- 24 percent prefer material gestures (money or gift cards that are useful);

- 10 percent say no reward is required if they can just get verbal recognition that they're doing a good job.[11]

While the trend for more frequent feedback-type information may have been elevated by millennials, they are also more in tune with how fast technology is forcing the way we work to change too. Feeling stagnant in a job without information to grow has been credited with being one of their greatest fears. Or it could be a fear of boredom. They aren't off here.

When anyone works in a void of information surrounding their own productivity, Forbes found that complacency descends fast, followed by boredom for many.[12] In contrast, learning what we are doing well fires up the brain to embrace all that it takes to keep doing it well.[13] Learning how others perceive us positively is exciting.[14] This is where feedback originally had great reception.[15]

Feedback helps us learn about ourselves through the eyes of another.[16] When the desire for improvement disrupts the balance of gaining examples of what goes well and areas for growth, we become dissatisfied and discouraged. Remember when you read about how discouraged Thomas was starting to feel in his work? It's because his boss was out of balance in his feedback. His boss's feedback concentrated on areas for improvement solely as if it offered a more competitive edge to do so.

Why bother with the fluff of what is going right? They still have a job, right? I've actually heard this said. This may have been the demise of the embrace of feedback.

When was the last time your heart quickened with fun anticipation when you heard, "I have some feedback for you?" Yep, didn't think so. When those words are offered, it's become a soft opening for "You need to improve." That saying is not fooling anyone.

And when we ask, "What do you think?" without any context, you are opening yourself up for feedback. Worse yet, there's a 50/50 chance that it's not the kind you want—or can use or even value.

It can also lead you down the Self-Improvement Trap.

Chapter 2 Questions

1. Do you feel you receive the recognition you deserve? How would you describe the recognition you do receive?
2. How have you experienced asking for open-ended feedback questions? Were your experiences different or similar to Carol's & Thomas's experiences?
3. What was your best experience hearing others share great things about you?

The Self-Improvement Trap

I used to wonder why other people walk the aisles of the self-help section of the bookstore. I mean, I've spent many an afternoon roaming the same aisles. I'm fascinated by what others are offering, their lessons learned, and how they came to write their book. I am always in awe of people overcoming challenges. I never expected to be faced with my own challenge and not find what I needed, until it happened. I don't think I'm alone here.

How often have you been frustrated with an instance at work in which you felt less-than? Or berated yourself for not stepping up, leaning in, asking better questions, or going the extra mile? That can happen as often as daily in fast-paced offices or when you are in a competitive industry, scrambling for clients between competitors. We get tired of that feeling, and we look for solutions. And we look for those solutions in the self-help industry.

The challenge becomes recognizing exactly what is frustrating you the most and then finding the resource that caters to that frustration point. Often it's not a one-size-fits-all approach, and you go through several different resources, only to realize your frustration feels so unique that there may not be a solution offered yet. Or at least you don't recognize it yet.

Challenges become so personalized that it's hard to just pick up any book and find the answer that works for you. And that may be what is making the journey feel so unique. Not all solutions work for everyone because everyone feels their issues are unique.

While I want you to realize how to celebrate what makes you unique, I know that finding a way to get this information is not unique. It's just not practiced—which leads us all running to the self-help section of a bookstore, YouTube channels, Facebook groups, and Meetup groups. These are all great resources. But they can lead us in circles, often facing more self-criticism than when we started.

Why?

Because in a genuine sense, when we do not feel like the outside world connects with us, we feel alone. And when we feel alone, we start picking ourselves apart with, the focus to change something to either fit in better with the others or feel better about ourselves. This internal thinking can become an awful trap. It is easy to get stuck here too. And it happens simply because we want to feel we belong.

We all want to belong, to be included—preferably somewhere inspiring. Which is why many of us follow someone who is an expert, entertainer, comedian, or simply someone who lifts us to explore an aspect of who we want to be—via self-help books, Facebook, YouTube, LinkedIn, and a multitude of social media platforms and community organizations.

I give you permission to stop the madness of seeking to be someone other than who you are. Instead, I'll give you information to step into loving who you are already made to be. We are all divinely made. Gallup can attest to that. With over eighty years of research in conducting their signature assessment in twenty different countries, all languages, age groups, and ethnicities, they found that due to our unique ways of thinking, given our own unique top-ten strengths, we are each 1 in 476 trillion.[17]

Yes! You are uniquely and divinely made.

There is fun and excitement in this.

To understand what makes you unique—so unique that your challenges feel unique too—is simply to explore the way we each think. And that affects the way we act, are motivated, react to stress, and what we seek to learn. When I learned this, I couldn't wait to learn more. I would love to know how to simply appreciate my gifts and not feel as if I must change to be happier!

I've learned more about my desire to hang out in the self-help section of the bookstore too. Turns out, learning is fun. Especially when it allows us to dream and be inspired to be who we know we can become—the hidden person we keep coaxing out in fits and starts.

Turns out, learning more about myself was more fun than getting information about what others thought about me via feedback. As shared in the prior chapter, feedback has taken a turn to be improvement driven rather than balanced with what is going right and where to grow.

And we don't look to it for reassurance. In fact, we avoid it, leaving us without any information to work with at all. I was curious why this was the case. Especially when we all become excited and energized when we learn what we are doing well. When we learn what others appreciate, we immediately start thinking of more ways to keep that going.

My questions stemmed around "Why do we pretend to want feedback when we don't really know how to get positive information from it? How could this be changed? What if we knew how to ask for feedback so we felt more in control of what information we could receive?" Like roaming around in the self-help section of the book story for information, I turned to research to see who else had asked these same questions—or at least similar ones.

That's when I came upon the book *Thanks for the Feedback: The Science and Art of Receiving Feedback Well (Even When It Is Off Base, Unfair, Poorly Delivered, and, Frankly, You're Not in the Mood)*. Long title—but it resonated. As I sat in a large conference hall having just heard Sheila Heen speak on how to handle conflict negotiation in organizations, this book she co-authored caught my interest. During her presentation, I revisited that dreadful performance-review lunch, as well as other times when someone would stop by and offer unsolicited feedback—some nice, some way off base, and some that I just wasn't in the mood to hear. Sitting in that conference center, I suddenly did not feel alone.

With that book I went on a journey I will never forget, and I want to share.

The Brain

I recently was able to see Sheila Heen speak at an HR conference. I appreciated that the approach to her research was the acknowledgment that our brains work for three distinct purposes:

1. storing memories while we sleep (which motivated me to get more sleep),
2. regulating our bodies, and
3. to protect us from risk.

Sheila Heen also explained that to intake information, the brain perpetually scans our environments in two ways to identify (1) how we are being loved (accepted/respected) and (2) where we can be learning (growing).[18]

For me, Love and *learn* take on a real meaning here.

Love encompasses the concepts of being accepted/respected here, as we don't look for romantic love in a repetitive way—we look for where we have the capacity to feel the love of human connections.

Learning is always connected to growing in knowledge, skills, new perspectives, and new behaviors. I will refer to these as "accepted/respected" and "growing."

Heen and Stone found that our brains are always in one of these states. Knowing this helped me understand how to start to alter the concept of my current, and often negative, relationship with feedback.

If the brain is looking for how to feel accepted/respected or where to grow next, then negative information doesn't fit in either of these categories. This could explain why negative information rolls around in our heads like a loose marble searching for a home.

Taking this into consideration, if we could reframe feedback into one of these two categories,

1. offering what we are doing great (the accepted/respected behaviors and performance)
2. and/or where to grow next (to learn)

this would put improvement into a new and helpful context and minimize the opportunity for unhelpful information or criticism.

This became a great way to gain information at work for me. This provided a better understanding of the way my brain worked, and I could evaluate where I felt accepted and respected—who made me feel that way, and you didn't. And I could evaluate the opportunities to learn more about other people and my work.

Supportive coworkers suddenly gained value to me, more than before. Coworkers often share success stories to bond over working together for a client, and they commiserate together when something unexpected happens or progress is slowed. We look for ways to bond and feel accepted and respected in all we do together. This is just one way work fulfills us on a relationship level. Turns out, you still need to know where to grow with other people too.

When we network, in person or via social media, we look for ways to relate (feel accepted) and do so with the intent to learn and grow in our connections. On social media, we might jump into discussions with like-minded people. Some we may know, while others are new people to meet. Doing so breeds feelings of connections, especially when our comments are accepted or celebrated.

While we actively scan our environments for information, we might also come across negativity in comments or opinions, which can set us back, causing many of us to temporarily withdraw from a particular conversation or our general interactions with a group. We do this to avoid becoming defensive or feeling rejected.

This is where I always counsel myself to be mindful.

Negativity short-circuits our thinking. It causes us all to minimize the positive and spotlight the negative. As a result, we require time to think through the negative comments, ponder them, roll them around in our brains. Seldom do we find a healthy home in our brain for negative comments, and often these can become triggers for irrational anger, frustration, or self-doubt.

When I realized how my brain constantly evaluated people and opportunities, it helped me review feedback with more insight. It also shed light on why I enjoyed reading self-help books to learn and grow.

Then I realized the trap I was in.

Avoid the negative, learn about something positive. Shun feedback, seek self-help. That cycle only gave me insights into other people's stories, not mine. This did not help me discover and embrace what makes me unique and an asset to an organization.

My approach needed a redirect.

Heen and Stone's work originated to understand how to facilitate positive feelings around feedback due to the negativity and conflict surrounding it. When Heen and Stone recognized that the receiver of the feedback always controlled what happens with the information given, they quickly redirected their approach too.

Instead of working to train people to give better feedback, as I and many fellow human resource professionals have spent countless hours doing, they shifted to help people understand how to ask for and receive feedback instead of waiting for it to be offered or relegated to an official performance review.

This creates a win-win result. Heen and Stone's work reveals that once someone understands how to effectively ask and receive feedback in a specific and useful manner, they immediately become better prepared to deliver meaningful feedback for others. My ears really perked up here. At the time I was researching this, I was an HR consultant, stepping into team engagement coaching, and this was a breakthrough idea.

Most companies still use performance reviews, and people rarely look forward to them. I now could offer a better way to engage people in performance feedback and find a new way to make feedback meaningful. I just needed to know more about why this worked.

Positivity and the Brain

Brent and I sat down together. I could see on his face that he was in a serious mood, probably ready to share the problems he was facing and wanted to discuss in our session. As I settled in across the table from him, I asked if we could start with him sharing what was going right. The contrast to what he was ready to share and what I was asking was evident on his face. Brent had to take a long pause before speaking, and when he began, it wasn't with the same confidence he possessed when he was laying out a problem. This was unknown territory. This was exactly why I asked this of him.

Shifting the brain from problem solving to appreciation takes energy. It's a lot like moving furniture. You push, you pull, you heave the heavy object. Then when you get in the right place, you feel exhilarated for having created a new space. This same feeling arrives when your brain shifts into appreciation mode too.

Within two minutes of talking, Brent's posture relaxed, and the lines on his face eased. He took time to breathe more evenly. He even smiled at one point when he shared a funny story from a peer. When he had finished sharing, he looked at me with a quizzical look. "I'm starting to see my problems I wanted to share in a different light, less dramatic than when I first arrived. How'd you do that?"

As a coach, I just asked a question—a type of question I know recalibrates the way we think.

I learned the value of this approach when reading about management practices aligned with positive psychology. The approach I discovered is now its own body of work in consulting change management, called "appreciative inquiry."[19] The ability to balance out the negative by first approaching what is already going right is the beauty of appreciative inquiry and a positive psychological approach.[20]

Taking time to appreciate what is going right balances out the weight of negativity due to the endorphins generated with positive thinking.[21] Endorphins are the chemicals that make us feel good, and when we feel good, our brains can transition more easily from idea to action. We think more clearly, our energy increases, and our focus becomes more optimized.

What Brent experienced was an ability to see what was going right and then reflect on the problems he had given so much weight to prior to our meeting. When he shared those problems, he was able to unpack them with better insights into who the problem affected, which solutions may work better, and why he had given them so much attention prior to our meeting. We discovered that the problems had more to do with how they made him feel and what was frustrating him the most. This allowed us to put more attention to the root cause for him faster than discussing the problems themselves. We often mask what we want to fix by trying to fix something else. This leads many of us back into the self-help trap. Therefore, assessing what is going right *first* is a useful tool. It reminds us to reframe our thinking. It also leads us to act faster.

In 2008 Barbara Fredrickson published research in the *Journal of Personality and Social Psychology* that revealed when people are exposed to film clips that elicit positive feelings, they are more likely to offer actionable ideas than those exposed to neutral or negative film clips. She found that when each group was asked to fill out a paper containing twenty spaces that all began with "I would like to . . ." the group exposed to watching film clips designed to produce feelings of joy or contentment gave the most responses. In contrast, those exposed to film clips that elicited negative feelings of sadness or fear gave the fewest responses. Participants who watched neutral content were also unable to respond with a lot of responses.[22]

In a work context, this has large profit-driven significance. It indicates that people who gain positive feelings from others or their work have more mental clarity and creativity and can foster a larger inventory of ideas and meet performance metrics more than those who struggle with fear and/or anger at work. Consider this when looking for ways to optimize performance, especially considering the desire for increased feedback in the workplace.

Fear and the Brain

Imagine you live in the mountains and are taking out the trash. As you open the garage door, you discover a bear close by, rummaging through the next-door neighbor's trash for food. You start frantically closing the garage door before the bear can realize you are the new food.

Then you stand there, frozen, breathing harder than normal, needing to collect yourself, trying to think clearly enough to take the next step. This takes longer than expected. You feel rattled for a long while. Your brain must deconstruct the reason it went into hyper-fear mode, help your body balance out your adrenaline, and find normal again.

This happened not only to me but my daughter too. We have a place in the Colorado mountains, and living with bears is a real thing. Just because it's a real part of life there doesn't make it any less scary when you're faced with it. Nor do we want to get comfortable with it. We need our response system to protect us for a reason.

This doesn't happen only when a bear threatens us. Stress and negative experiences do this to our brain *every time*.[23] Stress generates fight, flight, or freeze reactions to protect us. Then, when the danger has passed, it takes time to come out of this state. This might explain why when people get rattled by unexpected bad news, they can't think clearly. They don't immediately regain their full focus. And they can't pay attention to what others expect of them until they regain their composure. This can also occur when people get robustly negative or poorly delivered feedback that traumatizes their idea of success at work.

This was what was happening to me while I sat in my car, still in the parking garage after the performance-review lunch, trying to unpack everything that had happened and rebalance enough to drive home. And yes, I wanted to drive straight to a bookstore and look for how to avoid this situation in the future. This is what I call the self-help trap—when you are so rattled and unsure of yourself that you think someone else has more information than you have inside of you.

Unlike the self-help cycle, this book will offer you a way to go after proof of what you do well when you need that reassurance, plus control the negative and poorly delivered feedback and get well positioned to avoid the same paralysis associated with bad news.

It's time to step off the hamster wheel of perpetual self-improvement and go after

- proof of what you do well;
- the ability to control negative and poorly delivered feedback; and
- how to position yourself well to avoid the paralysis associated with bad news.

Shall we get started?

Chapter 3 Questions

1. Have you experienced a situation where, when faced with needing to solve a problem, you found yourself seeking information from the self-help industry?
2. Who was the most recent person to commend you for being unique in a positive way?
3. What impact did it have on you to read that your brain is always scanning for either where you belong or where you could grow?

The Curiosity Perspective

S tanding in the kitchen of our small military home following a dinner out with friends, my husband turned to me,
trying to be calm: "I have some feedback for you."

Warily I said, "OK."

Exasperation on his face, he said, "Honey, you just talk
too much!"

Stunned, I stood there, tears welling in my eyes.

What? I wanted to scream. *I've been home with young kids all
day, working from home, and trying to make it all work! I just needed
to have some adult conversation!*

Instead, I just looked at him, tears streaming down my face,
unable to speak. I felt embarrassed and hurt. Had I embarrassed
him in front of our friends? Had I embarrassed myself?

I thought back to the restaurant and thought, *Yep, I probably
did act like an attention-seeking sponge. I really wanted someone to
hear me. I was so tired of hearing the kids complain that I didn't even
ask questions. I must have been a fountain of words with no ears. Ugh!*

Unfiltered feedback is tough.

I know my husband loves me, yet he was so frustrated he
hadn't thought about how to tell me kindly. Of course, I needed
to be more aware. He had counted on me to be a decent conversationalist because I'm curious about other people. That night,
apparently, not so much. We were both frustrated.

Now we have the wisdom to encourage each other to grow.

Rewind to a year ago: I tried my new idea out on an easy conversation with my husband. I presented the context of the last time he saw me speak to an audience, and I asked my husband to share what he felt I did well. I was exploring this theory about finding a great way to ask this type of question and collect insights into what we do so well that we know what to honor whenever change is being considered. I was thrilled that it worked, and he shared something I never knew.

"The last time I came to see you speak, I saw you interacting with all the attendees. So effusive. Natural. As if you couldn't meet a stranger. I just was so impressed in how you engage with others when you enter a room. Don't ever change that—it's part of your charm."

I had totally let this event slip into the recesses of my memory. He had so easily provided me the context, what he observed, and an example of it. That example allowed me to see myself from his perspective. That was a huge learning moment for me, as I now recognize what he looks for and considers positive. The payoff for my curiosity was getting to feel great about something I do so naturally and yet had never known to be proud of.

When was the last time you were so genuinely complimented?

When was the last time you were curious enough to ask how someone else saw you?

Or better yet, when was the last time you were genuinely curious? Let's start there.

Was it when you met someone new and they offered details about their interesting career choice?

Was it to learn a new technology hack to make your life at work more efficient?

It could have been anything. That's the secret of curiosity—it engages your brain in growth. When your brain is engaged in growth, it feels good. And positive feelings end up being associated with learning. Here's the funny thing about learning—it gets maximized only when you are genuinely curious.

What I needed from researching how to ask for feedback was how to ask for positive feedback. Not only had I become curious, but curiosity started to pop up in research as well. Suffice it to say, curiosity was at an all-time high for me on this topic.

Dr. Kashdan, a professor of psychology at one of my alma maters, George Mason University, offers that curiosity causes us to look for the new and unfamiliar within something familiar.

Yes, I was looking for the new and unfamiliar within the familiar context of feedback. Kashdan often references this as expecting to learn something that opens new ideas and answers.[24] Learning is what our brain recognizes as growth, which positively engages the brain; thus, I eagerly referenced my journey as looking for the positive unfamiliar.

In his book *Curious? Discover the Missing Ingredient to a Fulfilling Life*, Kashdan shares his research on anxious children and the difference curiosity reveals. This is crucial to address because I'm going to offer you a framework to try, and anytime we try something new, anxiety can arise. Tapping into your curiosity will help you be more successful and have a much bigger payoff.

An analogy I found interesting was offered by Kashdan after working with children who reported high levels of anxiety.

Picture a pulley with a bucket on each end of a rope. One bucket represents anxiety and the other curiosity. When a child's anxiety bucket was full and became heavy, their curiosity bucket was empty and became too light to balance the weight of the anxiety bucket. Here I could picture the buckets like a seesaw—with one seat much higher than the other.

When Kashdan reported the results of children tapping into their curiosity, it was if their curiosity bucket started to fill up and their anxiety bucket started to empty, balancing them out.[25]

In Kashdan's exploration of curiosity as an outward-thinking activity, I found it in alignment with Heen and Stone's work. When we seek to know more, we look outside ourselves for information. When we dwell on what we can do better, what other people think of us, how we could do this or that—basically, when the subject of our interest is ourselves—we're engaged in inward thinking.

Reading Kashdan's work, I resonated with the idea that inward thinking triggers anxiety, self-criticism, and more negative emotions. I realized that when I am not learning anything new about myself, I tend to simply dwell on what I currently know.

Dwelling on what I currently know yet seeking new information often causes me to create my own misinformation—information that may not be true. And misinformation can warp our perspective. Yes, I've experienced this, and I bet you have too. When I doubt myself the most, if you ask me what I do well, I can't tell you—I lose my perspective.

Kashdan's findings suggest that using outward thinking—or curiosity—may be the healthiest thing we can promote within our own practice of conversation and to explore new perspectives about ourselves. When we become curious, we are motivated to learn. Motivation to learn prompts our brain to assimilate and understand how to use new information. As a result, we grow in knowledge.

You can't read the label from inside the bottle

I'm offering to help you grow in the knowledge of what you do so well, that you discover what not to change, even when change is needed. To do this you must be curious enough to look outside yourself for information.

Why? Because it is too hard to read the label from inside the bottle. Without others' perspectives, you have no way of understanding how people perceive you, what they admire about you, why they may enjoy working with you, or what helps you continue to get the promotion.

Curiosity is the only way to step into this adventure.

How do you do this without falling into the trap of perpetual self-improvement? It depends upon what you focus upon.

What Makes You Most Curious?

Are you more curious about what you do well—or what you don't do well?

To be able to communicate your value to the world at any given time, you need to gather the information about what you do well. You need to be *curious* about what you do well.

Yet we're not practiced at this. It could be because good news doesn't draw as much drama as bad.

Good News or Bad?

We don't see newspaper headlines declaring what everyone did right today. Why? Because good news doesn't sell as well as bad news. I was truly dismayed to see proof of this, as I'm a happy-ending, romantic-comedy, murder-mystery where-they-find-the-killer type of fan. Yet this is a proven psychological phenomenon.

In 2014, researchers Marc Trussler and Stuart Soroka published a study, conducted at McGill University in Canada, where they found that participants claimed to want to hear more good news than bad. Yet when put into a blind test that captured their eye movement upon reading news, they repeatedly read all the bad news before looking at the positive news. They concluded that, regardless of what people say they want, they want to know the bad news first.[26]

Psychological research provides two reasons for this.

First, our instincts for self-preservation requires us to look for anything unusual and/or threatening so we can protect ourselves and those we love. This is often why people gather around news screens for late-breaking news—to learn together and get a sense of what the crowd thinks all should do. This is helpful when needing to prepare for hurricanes and threatening weather patterns and life events that may result in harm, including war efforts. Finding solutions, saving one another from harm, and providing safe options to avoid destruction can pull us together. We often see the best in people during times of need.

But fatigue sets in too, so ongoing bad news can become detrimental to our health. Without the positive, we become anxious and depressed, often resulting in irrational thought.

Indeed, a constant diet of bad news does more long-term harm than good. Yet we still fixate on it. Tom Stafford offers that bad news may be a sign that we need to change our current actions to avoid danger—and we want to be the first to know so we can act.[27]

The second reason, according to Trussler and Soroka, is that our tendency to seek bad news first has to do with our reaction to bad news. They claim we tend to find bad news surprising because we usually view our personal lives with more positive, better-than-average outlooks.

Meaning we often see our current reality through rose-colored lenses—more specifically, we think the bad stuff won't happen to us. This may alter our ability to be open to views that are different than our own because the bad news just doesn't fit where we think it should.

Is the reason, then, that we shy away from seeking information, such as feedback, due to the unwelcome disruption of our own view of ourselves? Yet we still desire to know how we are doing so we don't become complacent, bored, or unchallenged. Conflicting desires that are connected.

I was finally connecting dots. If the desire to learn about how we can improve feeds our desire to learn and grow, would asking about what we do well feed our desire to feel accepted/respected?

Turns out—yes!

Balancing our desire for the positive creates a healthier backdrop for bad news when the subject is our own performance. So instead of shying away from the idea that bad or negative feedback is imminent or expecting only bad feedback, let's move into what Kashdan suggests—let's employ curiosity and proactively explore positive and new information.

I'm asking you to first implement curiosity so that you gain information that shifts your perspective. Gaining positive and new information about how others see us, how others enjoy working with us, and what we do that others see as positive will shift your perspective. Not only about learning how others see you positively, but what other people recognize and look for.

If this all sounds like I'm asking you to step into uncomfortable conversations . . . I'm not. I'm asking you to tap into the magic this opens for you. Unless you fear magic, then yes, I'm asking you to step into something potentially uncomfortable.

Here is where I found the magic. Rather than being uncomfortable, the feedback conversation became enjoyable—for both me and the other parties. Both find the information exchange positive, engaging, and meaningful, plus it helped build my own database of information that revealed my own unique superhero value.

To see yourself, you must not only believe in who you want to be, but you need to also look through the eyes of other people so you can see yourself as they view you—you will be amazed!

Chapter 4 Questions

1. Consider a time when you were curious: How did it feel to engage in your curiosity?
2. How do you behave when you feel accepted and respected—that is, when you belong?
3. How does your behavior change when you are unsure if you are accepted and respected?

When Did an ASK Mean So Much?

We know curiosity feeds your brain in a good way.
We know you say you want good news yet will run to read the bad news first—just in case zombies are really a thing.

Yet we know good news is the only way to collect insights about our strengths as seen by others.

This seems like a dilemma. Or is it?

Expecting bad news and receiving good news rarely works, since we've primed our brain to be on the defense and not the offense. This priming limits our capacity to "hear" the good news. If you change that and expect good news and hear bad news, it's equally destabilizing. How do we put the expectations of good news and the results of good news on the same page?

By asking in a specific way—because that's the magic you can control.

How Do You ASK for Such Magical Information?

First, you need to get curious about what you really want to know. Then you can ask and control the topic *and* control what gets delivered to you.

Here's What I Mean: Meet Shanda

Shanda works at a global IT firm and was passed over for a promotion that she felt she deserved. Others felt she deserved it too. The topic had come up again since the person hired for that role was looking to move on. I was interviewed and hired to coach her to explore how to prep for the role and interview with success to avoid getting passed over again.

One of the tools we put to use was conducting a customized 360 review: a review that allows fellow employees, direct reports, and supervisors to provide feedback in a formalized way that highlights what is going well and any areas for growth in someone's performance at work. I've included using the approach of asking with more clarity (which I provide you), and I've come away with a larger variety of helpful information than settling for simpler answers.

I encouraged Shanda to utilize the same approach to gain information firsthand from peers, past coworkers, friends, and family. My first question to her when we met after she completed her research was, "What did you learn that you don't need to change, even if you do get promoted?" She blushed, then she straightened, and she had a list that she had compiled. She learned that her peers, past coworkers, and her professional friends all felt she was a great communicator, that she was approachable, kind, compassionate, and helped others achieve results on time. She learned specific examples of when they saw this in action, and she now had a more vivid idea of what they appreciated and how they saw her, as well as the situations in which they had collaborated with her. This is no small amount of information. Her confidence increased exponentially as she learned how others appreciated her.

I asked her what she found difficult about this approach. She replied, "Only getting the first conversation started—then I was on a roll, and it was fun!"

Remember, the first conversations could easily be with a person you have an established relationship with. Plus, the foundation of the conversation is easily established using the context that elevates your curiosity. This framework provides you with solid information that reveals your own powers.

Your own Superhero Powers are made real by how they are seen by others.

The Framework for Crazy Good Info

I uncovered this framework when my research to train others to give feedback was turned on its ear by the work of Heen and Stone. After my big aha moment, I immediately ditched my training and turned to their research to form this framework for feedback! I was *not* expecting it, but that's what happened. It took one tiny sentence from great researchers to produce a huge perspective shift with big results in my work.

When any information is given that feels like feedback, the person with the power within that conversation is not the person providing the information—it's the receiver.

Here it is again. Ready?

> When any information is given that feels like feedback, the person with the power within that conversation is not the person providing the information—it's the receiver.

Meaning, that when anyone gives you "feedback," the power is in the results of that conversation, and the receiver has the power to create results—or *not*. And if the receiver controls what happens with any information offered, training people to give feedback suddenly felt pointless.

P-O-I-N-T-L-E-S-S.

My next thought was "Wow, I need to help people understand how to go after the information they WANT, WHEN they want it." Which means this book is about HOW to go get it.

How to get the information you need means you need to ask—but not just any ask. There is a rhythm to it, a system, and a purpose and intention. A Framework.

Your intention is to learn how others see you doing things that they like, they're proud of, they're impressed by, and that you are *not* being asked *to change*.

To see your Superhero Powers through the eyes of others, you need to gain information about yourself that you can use and repeat as well as grow and master.

When you find out the behaviors and actions you offer that others brag about, these are the very things you DO NOT HAVE TO CHANGE about yourself. And this is a big deal. Does that mean you can't change them? No. It allows you to relax, appreciate, and then decide whether to get better at doing those very things.

For example, when my husband shared how much he enjoyed how I engaged with people I meet, I will always remember that and excel at doing that very thing as often as possible. I can always get better too. I'm not stuck on just how I used to do it—improving is fun when I know what I already do well.

Using and repeating what you do that others enjoy will never fail you—if you recognize the context. So let's start there.

Step 1: Provide Context

When you ask anyone about any topic, you will have a better conversation when you state the context. Clarity is king in any conversation, especially to avoid the "What do you think?" trap that occurs when you don't provide context.

Context brings clarity.

If I hand in a report and merely ask my boss what I did right, she might say anything from "Great job of turning it in on time" to "Great colors on the data graphs." Neither answer is particularly helpful. But when we provide context, we frame the conversation to include the information we desire. When we're specific, we have control of the type of information we receive. When we guide and narrow the conversation this way, the other person is more likely to give useful information.

> For me, context is the key—from that comes the understanding of everything.
> —Kenneth Noland

Without context, even the feedback we receive could be unhelpful or negative. Providing context is essential to receiving the right information.

For example, you need to know if you are on track for a promotion. You want to understand how you are doing and what you can do more of to make sure a promotion is in your future. You can provide context around this topic. Here's how:

You to your boss: "I am interested in setting myself up for a promotion in the future" or "I'm curious to know what I currently do well now that helps set me up for a promotion in the future."

Keep Context Positive

If we frame the context in a positive way, the information we receive usually stays positive. If the context is not provided, the other person feels they have license to give you their opinion, and that could be negative. When I ask for information, I'm not giving someone license to be negative. However, if I do not provide context, that's exactly what I could get.

Some people feel that, when you ask them for information, they are obligated to provide something of value, which is often an area for improvement and is often received as a negative to the person hearing it. Without providing specific context, you may be opening the door to receiving information that is not as helpful as you'd like.

Context and clarity are key to lifting each other up. Clearly defined context keeps the door securely connected to the framework of the context offered. When done well, this tends to limit negative input or output.

> The biggest emotion in creation is the bridge to Optimism.
> —Brian May

Step 2: Ask for One Thing

The next gift you can provide someone is to reduce the information down to one thing. Heen and Stone's work revealed that when we want to gain important information, asking someone for the one thing automatically forces their brain to conjure up the most important piece of information.[28] For example, if someone asked me, "Can you tell me what I did well in the last meeting?" and the number of specific details was not provided, I may list off one thing or ten, leaving the person who asked to wonder which one was the most important. To save the confusion, we need to understand our brains.

One Thing and the Brain

Oddly enough, the brain can only concentrate on one thing at a time, good or bad. There is a body of research that identifies when the brain is given more than one piece of information, the brain immediately weighs both pieces of information equally.[29] Turns out, the brain needs to evaluate each bit of information one at a time. When forced to consider multiple pieces of information without comparison, the brain often neutralizes both and selects the one that is preferred. Receiving more than one piece of positive feedback at a time is no different.

Think about the last time someone complimented you on a singular thing. You were able to think about it and appreciate it. Now think about the last time someone complimented you on several things at once—your appearance, your timeliness, your choice of car. You might have immediately discounted the praise because it was too much at once. You might even have thought the person was nuts or wanted something from you later. The bottom line is that your brain didn't get the chance to value one compliment more than the others. If you discount one, your brain tends to discount them all, creating a completely lost opportunity for you to feel great about the one thing the person noticed but lumped into a set of other compliments.

Without specifics, your perspective never changes. Perspective is key here. Gaining a positive piece of information provides clarity on what you do well—at least enough to honor it and not change it until you want to.

Always ask for one thing. "Can you tell me the one thing I did really well in the last meeting?"

What if there are two things?

Finding one thing is a simple concept, but you will feel challenged to stick to just one thing. While you may be tempted to receive more positive information in the same conversation, you are doing a disservice both to yourself and the other person.[30]

Your goal of finding out as much as possible at one time will backfire, open the door to negative remarks and criticism, and allow the information to get lost without properly filing it in your brain. This makes the conversation ineffective for both parties.

While the goal of maximizing the opportunity to collect new information all at once seems logical, you end up devaluing each new piece of information, as your brain weighs them all equally. Then you don't get to take the time to unpack and invest in each piece of information.

Here's a quick example that helps me to stick to one thing.

Meet Balancing Bert. Bert loves to offer both pro and con information. He feels the need to balance the positive with the negative information. Don't let him. Here's how to do this nicely.

"Hi, Balancing Bert. Last week, after I presented my report to the team, Smiling Susan in accounting asked me to give it again next quarter. Since you were also there, I'd like to know what to keep constant as I prepare for next quarter" (context). "Could you tell me one element of that presentation that I did well?" (the one thing).

Balancing Bert answers.

You: "Please tell me what that looked like from your perspective" (the example).

Bert: "But wait—I have another point I think you'd like."

You: "I'm sorry. I know it must be valuable, but I can handle only one piece of information right now. Can I circle back to you when I'm ready for more?"

Since our brains can handle only one piece of new information well, it's wise to give them the time, energy, and thought necessary to integrate information fully.

Take information in small amounts. Enjoy the information you receive. Think about it from different perspectives and in different settings and situations. Honor the things you are doing right by letting them soak into your memory.

I practiced this technique recently with my writing coach. When I told her one of the things she did well and then gave an example of how she was doing it, she beamed. Then she said she was going to take time to let it soak in. Later, she said this "one thing" meant more to her than any other compliment she received this year.

Step 3: The Perfect Ending—Ask for an Example

To help the conversation take on a meaningful turn for both, ask for an example. Asking for an example of how the other experienced it, how they saw it, or when they saw it allows them to share information from their own perceptions and viewpoint. It is a priceless piece of insight, as you now get to see how they perceive your actions and work.

Meet my daughter, Colleen.

Me: "Hi, hon. Can I ask you a question about our last vacation together?" (Context: we had gone to Ireland where I was speaking, and she came to help.)

Colleen: "Sure, Mom."

Me: "When we were traveling together, what was the one thing that I did that helped you have a great time?"

Colleen: "Hmmmm, let me think. I think it was your openness to seeing the good in whatever happened."

I didn't really know what she meant, and even if I had, I would still encourage all of us to ask for an example.

Me: "Wow, that's interesting. Can you give me an example of what you mean?"

Colleen: "Sure. I mean, we hadn't planned anything after your speaking engagement, so we were winging it, and you rolled with it. We planned as we went, and it wasn't always smooth, yet you helped limit my complaining by reminding me what was going right. I appreciated that, and it helped me calm any anxious thoughts, since you were not getting anxious either."

Examples are as important as context. Asking for an example can give multiple levels of benefits. Often, the most surprising information comes from this last part of the conversation.

There are three benefits. The first benefit is that you get to hear firsthand what your success looks like from another's perspective. We usually have no idea how others see us. Understanding how others view us is vital to increasing our self-awareness.[31] Even those who have suffered a brain injury often need to gain information from others to repair their own self-awareness as they heal.

We will always need to increase our self-awareness if we want to be successful. Doing so opens us up to increased confidence and helps us look at opportunities with more courage and continue what we do well more consistently.[32]

Second, asking someone to provide an example is no different than asking them to share a story. In a report generated by Sole and Wilson (2002) of Harvard University, sharing information through a story makes the information more manageable and absorbable.[33] It also generates an emotional connection. When emotions are evoked, the connection between the brain and the knowledge being offered provides more meaning.[34]

The third benefit is that the other person may now become more invested in your success. People enjoy contributing to success. When they help you understand what you do well, they enjoy feeling as if they've had a part in your success. This is often why many successful people become mentors. They want to pay it forward by sharing their stories to help others. Look for these people. They will be accustomed to sharing the positives, and they'll help you understand why it matters to your success.

The Goal: One Conversation at a Time

The goal is to always be in control of the context you offer, aware of the one-thing limit, and to gain an example of how the other person sees you. Continue to do this with family, friends, and coworkers. Ask about everything. Soon you'll have a vast array of things you do well and don't have to change.

Word of caution: limit your questions to one at a time, and provide space for the answers to have time to be appreciated by your brain. To be clear: Do not pummel one person with a ton of questions to gain a multitude of information—even when tempted. This is not efficient for your brain or enjoyable for the other person. Ask about one thing, within one context, and gain one example and move on. One conversation is best. You can always make this a repeat experience—just space them out and revel in their uniqueness each time.

Gaining a collection of one thing you don't have to change in the vastly diverse areas of your life is an amazing adventure. It will also help you understand your value to your current employer, or when you're interviewing for a new role, or deciding when to apply for a coveted position at work.

It will help you see how your family values you and how your friends view you. It could even explain why those people interact with you the way they do. It will help you keep perspective on what to value most about yourself, instead of comparing yourself to others or the latest social media trends.

I have found this observation priceless when challenging clients on what they need to know rather than want to know. One might think that what they want and need would be the same, yet Ryan's words come through loud and clear when we realize how we are measuring ourselves. This is crucial when we are setting the context for a meaningful conversation.

When you ask a client to tell you the one thing you've done that has made a positive impact for them, make sure you communicate the context clearly to the client. That way you can ask for, and receive, information that aligns with what matters to you, the company, and your career.

> "People want so desperately to matter, and yet they measure themselves by things that don't."
> —Author and Media Strategist Ryan Holiday

For example, if you value excellence in customer service, this is the context you use when asking for information. You can simply share that you would love to understand more about your delivery of customer service because you strive for excellence (context); could they please share with you the most meaningful element of customer service you've offered that has made a positive impact in their customer experience (the one thing). Then ask if they can share an example of that experience.

You may have noticed this has an element of market research to it. Meaning you could ask all your clients, past and present, the same thing to gather a collection of examples of your customer service delivery. This helps you understand how the world sees your customer service excellence, and these testimonials not only evaluate your value, they allow you to market what matters in your success too. This has the added benefit of elevating your brand, which is priceless.

By simply asking for information in a specific format, you can gain amazing knowledge about yourself. This is instrumental for your personal satisfaction and confidence at work too.

Chapter 5 Questions

1. To learn one thing that you do well, and could continue to do, can you name five people you could start asking?
2. Let's get your ASK ready. Write your answers to the following, and practice:
     a. What is the context you want to use?
     b. What is the one thing you want to explore?
     c. How will you remind yourself to always ask for an example?

Why @ Work

When you find out how you impact others positively, collecting examples and details of what you do well provides feelings of exhilaration. I encourage you to enjoy this feeling. Learning something new and positive elevates your capacity for new knowledge and problem solving.

The Mirror Lies!

As I began writing this, I faced week six of the recommended shelter-in-place quarantine of the 2020 COVID-19 pandemic. On this morning I found myself staring into the mirror. Feeling isolated, alone, confused, and directionless, as if my goals were purposely hiding out on vacation somewhere and I couldn't see clearly in my fog. I coach people past this very thing, and yet here I was, stuck in a similar fog, experiencing the challenge firsthand.

My mind spiraled into the world of the "shoulds":

I should be going after more business right now.
I should be more actively reaching out to others.
I should be using this time to get prepared for the quarantine release.
I should be caring more for myself
I should be working out more.
I should . . . I should . . . I should . . .

I could feel the anxiety and the stress building and looming through the fog. I have found that the word "should" is simply a way to convey frustration, and when we fall into this habit, it hijacks our ability to think clearly. And here I was in the middle of my brain being hijacked by the very "should" I help others avoid! Of course, noting this didn't make it any easier to shut it up. *Ugh. Stop the "shoulding"!*

The person looking back at me from the mirror was staring, expectantly, my "should" self-talk falling into a swirl of made-up lies—ideas and thoughts conjured up without the right information, a warped perspective of not being enough.

"Stop right there. This is not helpful." I spoke back to myself in the mirror.

I knew I needed to pull from my brain what I coach my clients to do.

I moved toward my office and grabbed the file. The file called *Superhero*. No, I do not have X-ray vision, the ability to float and fly, or to disappear (though I think it would all be cool!).

What I have is my own secret file of testimonials, emails, and thank-you letters that remind me of my skills and instinctual, natural strengths that help me be successful with my clients. And right then I needed a refresher of those examples to bring me back to embracing my best self so I could move forward and get back into my best life.

While it may sound slightly egotistical to have a file labeled *Superhero* full of testimonials, attagirl notes, thank-yous, or printed-out emails, it is not. It is for righting the mental ship when the "should" storms hit. It is reminding you of what is going right—which kicks the brain in the right spot to produce the feel-good endorphins that help balance and neutralize the cortisol from the stress of the "shoulds." Everyone needs one—I wish I could include a file folder with this book for you.

The Superhero File

As I opened the file and started to reread emails and testimonials, I zipped back in time to each interaction. These emails and testimonials were sent from people I had coached, taught via webinar, facilitated a workshop for, or simply offered the phone call when they were in need. I was reminded of what I do best.

These bits of information I was reading didn't all just come out of the goodwill of the writers. While I love the unexpected email or testimonial that highlights a strength, most I asked to provide because I know I need to see my strengths from others' perspectives. How did I do it? How did I create my Superhero File?

I often ask those I coach a version of the following questions in a conversation or in follow-up materials:

> **Context:** "It has been an honor to see you succeed within our time together, and I'd love to gain two pieces of information from your perspective." (Again, this is a version—it is often more customized.)
>
> **One thing:** "What is the one thing that we explored together that provided the biggest aha moments for you?"
>
> **Example:** "Can you share with me an example of how and/or what actions you are excited to take moving forward?"

I've now included this in my business practice and as part of my customer-experience processes. This is where a survey can be a part of your practice, and it can be a great practice in conversations as you do follow-up. Gathering examples of having made a positive impact helps me honor what I offer the world, things I don't have to change even when I know change will be desired or needed as I grow in my own life.

The Perspective Shifts

When your mood, emotions, or the stuff of life attempts to hijack your day, reminders of your positive impact on others shifts your perspective back to a healthier balance and rebuilds your sense of purpose. When you learn what you are doing right, this theory of what you do well shifts from a flimsy idea to the foundational element of you at your best. It becomes the building blocks for finding solutions. Sure, you still can grow in any area you choose, but at least you know what not to eliminate in how you contribute to others.

When we sense a problem, we often spend way too much time thinking about it and stress over it—like that day when I was stuck staring in the mirror after being isolated for weeks on end. Having a plan of action is helpful. On that day I was able to put my plan of action into motion—even if it was to just open a file and read. It helped me reset, and it can help you too.

Positive psychology and appreciative inquiry have found merit in helping individuals and teams neutralize the stress of new problems by exploring all that is going right *first*.[35] There are two ways to use this concept.

1. List what is going right about the topic and context surrounding any new problem
   Example: A problem arises with how the client is receiving expected project portions.
   To list what is going right will keep the client focused on the positive and allow both you and the client to communicate clearly on what is expected and how to achieve that without guessing. This helps avoid the "fireman" approach of hosing down everything and elevates your professional relationship to one of critical analysis and faster results.

2. List all that is going right as far as current actions/results before tackling how to handle a new project or a new element of an existing project.
   Example: A new addition to a project has just been added that affects an existing project portion. Assessing all that is going right in the existing project keeps it front of mind when assessing how the new project portion needs to be implemented. The ability to go to the client with any information

about what will be affected—that they currently like in the project—will keep everyone working toward what they want to keep or change with more open communication toward the end goal. This helps avoid all assumptions that the new addition automatically overrides the existing project portions. New isn't always what is desired if what works is incorrectly eliminated. This approach keeps everyone more informed.

This practice often prevents the escalation of unnecessary stress and drama when things need new solutions. This sets the stage to solve the problem by identifying what is being done well and what does not need to change as new ideas are offered. This has also helped facilitate innovation faster too.

Meet Daniel

"Daniel, what's your biggest challenge right now in the interview process?" I asked.

"Well," he replied, "I'm struggling with how to describe a weakness without feeling like it would reflect negatively on me. I mean, how do you talk about a weakness when you're trying to showcase your strengths to get a job?"

His frustration was written all over his face.

"Daniel, what do you consider one of your weaknesses?"

He looked baffled and shrugged. "I don't know. I mean, we all have them."

"OK, then, what have you been criticized for at work?" I countered.

"Oh, I got criticized recently for how impatient I get when anyone on my team is late to a meeting. Apparently, I get short with them during the meeting. I guess it shows that I'm mad at them for being late."

"How do you normally handle your own time management?"

"I am punctual!" His chest puffed a little. "I was in the military. If you're only five minutes early, you're late. I respect the time of others and have always loved being early enough to settle in on time. I really don't understand how other people think they aren't inconveniencing others when they show up either right at the start of a meeting or late. It does tick me off. I just didn't realize it was so obvious to others."

"Well, this gives us an opportunity to flip this in a good way," I offered.

He looked up.

"You feel your time management is a strength, right?"

"Yes."

"But how you treat other people who don't have the same strength has been described to you as a weakness, right?"

"Yes," he answered cautiously.

"So your strength, when pushed upon others, has a negative effect, and others become frustrated and critical," I confirmed.

He waited, as if holding his breath.

"We can work with this." I smiled.

"I'm all ears," he said.

For the interview, I knew we needed to position Daniel to be able to talk positively about this perceived weakness. We discussed ways to not push his time needs upon others unnecessarily and to instead build in ways for those who have a different concept of time to still be successful. That was when he had a solution-oriented aha moment. He decided to clearly communicate the meeting's defined start time with a built-in social time scheduled beforehand. This approach would offer those who need to socialize, and settle in, a designated time to do that, while those who prefer to show up right when the meeting is supposed to start know to shut up and sit down, not chitchat.

He gave this a try at work.

"Daniel, catch me up on your meetings," I asked at our next meeting.

"I couldn't believe it," he said, shoulders relaxed, a smile on his face. "It worked like a charm. Did you know that I had the nickname of the 'Time Police'?" He laughed.

"After the first meeting went so well, everyone saw me relaxed and proud that the meeting had started on time. A couple of my team members came up and thanked me for communicating this new time format. They shared that while they wanted the meetings to start on time for themselves, they really wanted them to start so I wouldn't be so impatient. That's when I learned about my nickname. *Ha!* Who'd've thunk it!" He grinned shyly.

This success energized him to then think about other feedback he had received, in a way he could elevate his leadership style with more insights. I encouraged him to go back and chat with others on his team using the ASK Framework.

- Set the context (e.g., the new meeting time setup).
- Ask for the one thing they appreciated about it.
- Then ask for an example of how implementing it works for them.

The ASK Framework would allow his team to answer with specifics. If the meeting time setup doesn't work for them, they may share that as well. Using the ASK Framework allowed Daniel to collect the perspectives from others, which he would have otherwise never gained.

While Daniel was learning more about what he was doing right at his current role, he was also practicing for upcoming interviews.

I use frameworks often, and I have two specific ones for interview answers. I coached Daniel in how to frame what to share. And when the prospective employer interviewed him, he was ready to address questions about sharing a weakness. Daniel framed his answer to share how his strength of time management was thought of as a weakness due to it being used with limited insight. He then shared how he'd implemented a new meeting schedule to mini-mize the negative impact on others and provided examples from his team on the positive impact this change provided. He shared how this experience prompted him to develop new lessons on time-management agility when training new managers on his team.

Daniel was able to successfully communicate his strength and the experience he now has on turning the negative perceptions of his time management into a productive conversation for teams to get meetings done on time. While he wasn't offered the first position, he was offered a better position shortly afterward. He was over the moon when he told me the news.

When someone learns what they do well, it's invigorating.

Daniel never had to change his relationship with time. This was something he had been commended on while in the military, and it had served him well. What was a stressor and becoming a problem was his frustration when others didn't have the same relationship with time. His stressing had frozen his ability to think from a different perspective. His preferred form of time management turned out to be something he got right; it just had been applied in the wrong way. To get his team on board was to understand how other people valued their time differently and to make minor adjustments in how to get along.

Reframing his time management as something he got right allowed him to open his thinking to solve the perceived weakness problem he first brought up. This is the magic of identifying what is going right *first*. It excites the creative juices in the brain. This works for you as an individual, and it is amplified when used on a team.

> Never view your challenges as a disadvantage. Instead, your experiences in facing and overcoming adversity is one of your biggest advantages.
> —Michelle Obama

Chapter 6 Questions

1. When you read about my Superhero File, could you imagine how a similar file could help you?
2. How could you use the ASK method to help you collect information to add to your own Superhero File? (ASK Framework: context—one area of focus/question, one example.)

The Ninety Days of Magic

Daniel's success at interviewing meant that he would be starting a new job. I asked what his plans were to elevate the first ninety days of his new role. He was surprised to hear me bring it up. He confessed he had put little thought into the first ninety days. He was still happy about his selection and remained psyched to get started, without putting thought into next steps. How often we fall into this trap.

I asked him what he knew about the company's work expectations of his role. He pulled out the job description and then paused. "I don't know exactly yet. I expect I will learn that once I get on the job."

"You may."

Then I asked if he'd like to put a plan together to optimize his first ninety days. With a ninety-day plan he would feel confident in his role and know more about how his role fits in with the organization's goals after his first quarter of employment. Even while learning the new elements of his new job, the culture, and other expectations, he would have his own plan to put into practice and use as a guideline to set the stage for intentional success instead of default.

Few people think like this when they get hired in a new organization, yet frustrations often start with unmet, unshared, or unclarified expectations within the first month. This often occurs on both sides—the boss and the employee.

When people do not thrive at work, it can be for a variety of reasons; however, it's often because they do not know the expectations, the expectations change too often, or the expectations are miscommunicated—or lost—by changing leadership.

Every person who goes to work, goes to work to be successful, to be paid a fair wage, and to use their talents. Therefore, asking about expectations is a necessary part of having a great work experience. An ideal time to start asking and collecting testimonials about how your skills, natural strengths, and talents positively impact those around you is before starting a new job. This way you are practiced enough to start asking similar questions to help you be successful your first ninety days in your new job.

The Best Ninety Days

I get sad when I see new employees flounder. A new employee is most vulnerable in the first ninety days.[36] In these days, they must learn the spoken and unspoken rules of the office, the office culture, and employee expectations, in addition to the new job they have just been hired to do. When employees flounder, it is often simply due to differing communication styles. A new manager or leader is no different, as their title, job description, and role expectations change too.

To minimize chances of floundering, it is critical to have an established and robust onboarding program.[37] Without it, many companies have difficulty retaining employees or promoting successful management. In those critical first months, communication is important so the new employee or leader can understand what to prioritize to be successful. Without that communication, the responsibility to succeed falls completely to the new employee. This can be daunting and discouraging.

Which is why I get excited to share this framework for gathering information. It not only helps you gather information on how others see your strengths in action, it is useful to gather intel to *be* successful too.

Asking Matters

The goal is to give you control on how to *be* successful as a new employee. To do that, I'm giving you the easy framework to ask others what you are doing that is working in your first days. This presents a positive conversation and shows your openness to connect with others (who are also your new coworkers).

This is such a gift to give your coworkers. They get to feel valued because you've asked for their opinion and insights. In your first days, they'll have more compassion, give you more assistance, and work more to help you succeed than in any other time in your career. Start the habit of asking about things that matter.

Ask what you are doing that works and what you can learn. This lets them see you are proactive and interested in success and that you value their thoughts and feelings. You can use this same technique to understand what to learn, especially concerning expectations.

Digging Deeper and Continuing the Conversation

Learning what matters is equally important to learning what is expected of you at work, in your relationships, and in your life. However, the things that matter to you at work may not match your employer's expectations. Knowing both will help you navigate your work life with solid critical thinking.

First, ask about all the general expectations of your new role: expected results, timelines, and relationships to develop to be successful in the role.

Here's an example:

- **Context:** "I'm new in this role and would like to set myself up for success. I realize part of that is understanding expectations."
- **One thing:** "What is the most important expectation I need to concentrate on understanding now?"
- **Example:** "Can you give an example of how you see me succeeding at that?"

Then in a week or two, ask what you are doing that works in meeting those expectations. You can ask this same question of many different people and start to get a well-rounded view of expectations from different perspectives. This helps you understand what matters to others. As a bonus, everyone you talk to now feels you value them. When you help people feel as if they matter, you start to matter to them too. It's a gift that gives back.

The Bottom Line Always Matters

When you reach out for information, either about the impact you already provide or what you could learn, keep in mind the outcomes that are a priority to your organization.

Outcomes connect directly to the bottom line of every company. Results are measured, data collected, strategies for success developed, and initiatives put into action—all based on the bottom line. When you become aware of the outcomes, you learn why you matter, why they have made a position for you, and how the company's expectations connect to your success. Do not be afraid to ask about outcomes. Here's one way a new employee can get right to the bottom line with the ASK Framework:

- **Context:** "How does our department's effort connect to the company's overall outcome goals?"
- **One thing:** "What number-one outcome does our work directly affect?"
- **Example:** "Can you give me an example of ways our efforts have affected that outcome in the past?"—or "How is our current work connected to our growth strategy?"

Do not shy away from asking about anything that links your daily efforts to the organization's success. It will matter that you show interest. Let others know you care that your work matters. If you don't get a satisfying answer the first couple of times you ask, ask in other ways.

When you know what you do that works, or helps others work, for the organization's success, you will have the courage to stick with it when the work gets tough, the days get long, and the problem and solutions get harder.

Go Global—It Matters

Learning what outcomes are affected by your own work, that of your department, or even of your entire organization is a smart step. Take it a step further and consider the bigger picture—how your organization connects to the world. Considering global outcomes allows you to connect the value of external influences—such as stock market returns, oil prices, terrorist activity, and weather—to internal activities.

When you wonder how the news will affect your organization, start a conversation about it when you get to work: "What is the one thing we do to protect ourselves from events like this?"

Connecting your work to global outcomes provides you with a sense of purpose, insight, and productivity. Offer someone else the one thing they do that contributes to the success of the team, department, organization, and the world. This can increase production, retention, and engagement. Connecting people to their purpose is always one thing that matters. We were all created with purpose and for the greater good.

The purposes of a person's heart are deep waters, but one who has insight draws them out.
Proverbs 20:5 NIV

Chapter 7 Questions

1. Ninety days is a span of time that is scientifically significant when adapting to anything new. Using the ASK Framework is something new that will serve you well. What area of your own work life makes you curious enough to start the process?

2. How will asking these questions benefit your participation within the organization?

ASK the Team

Heidi works in a government role and has a team she works hard to keep focused. She attended a workshop I offered on the ASK method, and we were connecting as a follow-up. Heidi shared an experience that brings home the value of paying attention to new team members and integrating the ASK method with what is going right for the team. The new team member was Sam.

"I think my office is getting sick of Sam." Heidi sighed. "He's only worked with us for four months, but he just won't stop talking about his old office! If he offers one more idea with 'You know, my old office had this really great idea I think would work here,' I might scream."

"Why?" I asked with a slight laugh. "Ideas are great!"

"When we get to hear about the ideas, they do sound great—but then he won't let us use any of them when we try and adapt them to fit our needs. It's so weird!" she said, shaking her head.

"What are you going to do?"

"Well, I have to do something. The other team members are starting to ignore him, and I can tell it's getting rough for him to handle. He does good, solid work, and while I think he's trying hard to fit in, he's starting to shut down and not interact as much anymore."

"Can I offer a few ideas of my own?" I asked.

"Yes, please! I'm a little too close to the situation here to have my own ideas these days."

I shared my idea of helping Sam find out what he did well in the eyes of others to help build more trust. And we discussed various ways to get Sam to open up more with Heidi.

Heidi later shared the following:

Heidi sat Sam down and used the ASK Framework in her conversation.

"Sam, given that you are new on the team, what's the one thing that has been exciting for you?"

Sam offered that he enjoyed his team and loved the work. Heidi then asked Sam to offer an example of a great experience he's had so far. While he shared, Heidi obtained a much better picture of how Sam saw aspects of the team.

Heidi then started a new conversation to understand more. She used the ASK Framework to start and then used two new approaches I'd offered her, to dig deeper.

> **Context:** "Sam, you came to work here from what sounds like a great company," Heidi started.
>
> **One thing and an example:** "You offer a lot of great ideas and yet won't let our team benefit from taking ideas that might work for us and innovating them to fit our needs."
>
> **Follow-up questions:** "What are you expecting to see happen when you offer ideas but won't let us alter them to work here? How would you like the team to respond?"

Heidi wanted to understand what was motivating Sam to offer the very ideas the team wanted to use but were frustrated when Sam wouldn't offer more information.

What followed was a conversation that then allowed Heidi to ask Sam to offer which parts of his ideas he thought would truly work and which wouldn't now that he knew the team better. After about an hour discussion, he and Heidi picked out which parts of his ideas would be exciting to experiment with to fit the team's needs. Sam was eager to get the team together and share what he and Heidi had discussed.

Heidi started the team meeting with the context. Before Sam's input, she had a request. She wanted everyone to share one contribution Sam brought by being on the team. As people offered how positively they viewed Sam's contributions and how much he added to the productivity and results, Heidi noticed Sam relaxing. She followed up with asking everyone to share an example of how they saw Sam contributing. She watched Sam's face as he took in the information—an appreciation and calm confidence started to show.

She then offered the real reason for the meeting and handed over the discussion to Sam. Sam was slow to speak; he was really moved by the positive things the team had said. What followed was a full disclosure of how he had offered his old company's ideas out of a desire to be helpful but then worried that the ideas wouldn't work, so he would pull them back at the last minute. He realized now how frustrating that must have been for them. This team meeting was to offer the best parts of his ideas and let the team have them. He was excited to see the team take them forward.

When Heidi finished telling me this story, she had to admit that she was more excited to work with Sam after this experience, and she was thankful to continue moving forward with the team. Sam and the team had responded so positively to her using the ASK Framework that it was becoming more of a practice for her, even several weeks after the workshop.

I thanked her sincerely for sharing. Even though I know this approach works, it's always great to hear someone's positive experience.

Pointing It Out Works

Without fail, by pointing out what others offer as positive contributions, the recipient gets to fully step into being their best self through the eyes of others. Heidi knew that Sam probably needed some of the right attention after such a rocky start, and her plan worked brilliantly.

Capturing what you do well and what others hope you don't change moving forward isn't just a self-involved exercise. You can put this into action for others as well.

When asked to provide information about others, you can now offer insights into what you see as their strengths. This allows you to offer up the context so they know what you are referencing, the one thing you admire, and an example as a snapshot of their strength in action—plus, it feels great to lift other people up. Win-win!

Strengths

Strengths are defined as how you naturally think and what behaviors are natural for you.

What you learn by asking how you positively impact others provides insightful examples of your strengths in action. Take note of which strengths are offered and who sees them. Pay attention to which strengths are recognized at work or at home. This information will give you a great sense of how others depend upon you, enjoy the strengths you offer, and what they may credit you for on a team.

If you do not have close family or coworkers nearby to explore a conversation about what you offer, there are assessments that are highly validated in providing insights into behaviors measured as strengths. While there are many different assessments, I have a personal preference for Don Clifton's Strength Finder assessment,[38] as it has proven the test of time across cultures, languages, ethnicities, and all age ranges. It's a great assessment to start the conversation around strengths, and once it's unpacked, it's often easy for everyone to recognize whom to ask because they see those strengths in action.

Why Is There Friction?

Your individual strengths will consistently show up in a variety of ways as you work together with others, individually or on a team. Certain strengths urge others to action. Others provide input, ideas, innovation, and creativity. Still other strengths involve recognition, significance, and reward. With different strengths, everyone sees a problem with a different lens, a different set of expectations, a different motivating purpose, and the accompanying solutions. Therefore, individual strengths may initially appear to cause or contribute to chaos. The first response to causing friction is to shut down.

Hang tough.

Good Innovation Is at Stake Here

Remember, every single person gets up every day to be their best self. When certain strengths are at extreme opposites, viewpoints and actions will clash and cause unexpected friction. Friction, while natural, is only because there is limited appreciation for opposite strengths. But opposite strengths create diversity of thought. Diversity of thought is exactly where innovation begins. Friction isn't the only way to see how people are opposite.

Things Do Not Always Look the Same

I recently attended a session on diversity.[39]

"Please look at the variety of objects in the center of the table, and write down what it makes you think of, nothing more," asked the moderator, and she uncovered a collection of unrelated objects on our table.

These were not unfamiliar objects but, rather, everyday items like an apple, a baseball, and some fruit. You might think many of us would come up with similar thoughts or memories: apple pie, baseball games, picnics. Yet the diversity of answers showed us that each person had a different lens. It was jaw dropping how differently we each saw the collection of items, and it was a direct reflection on how diverse our viewpoints, mental processes, gender, age, and culture influenced our perceptions.

Diversity of thought and vision brings innovative solutions.[40] The different strengths within each person shapes our thoughts and colors our vision. Optimizing personal strengths maximizes the team too. Each team member will see problems differently. They will want to ask different questions, be motivated by different thoughts, and will see solutions differently because of their individual strengths.

Which is why learning how others perceive us matters. It reveals to us our strengths, characteristics, and behaviors in ways we would have never seen for ourselves. Find out how you positively impact others as soon as possible. The added benefit is it will prompt you to appreciate and value how different others are as well.

> Great things in business are never done by one person. They're done by a team. —Steve Jobs

Plumbers and Baseball

Each person is unique. We usually appreciate this in unexpected ways. Take baseball. It is rare for a coach to throw an established team of players out in the field, have everyone throw the ball to each other, and then yell at them all for not being great pitchers.

We know that only a few will be great pitchers, while others will make better infielders, outfielders, and catchers. While it helps if all players can hit the ball well, having the players know what they each do well on the field helps the entire team succeed. When members know where to focus their contributions and their strengths, the entire team moves forward quicker. Ask any player who's made it to the big leagues—it takes a team of individually unique players, who know how to optimize one another's talent, to win a team award.

In contrast, take plumbers. Having just gone through some home remodeling, I have come to appreciate the talents of different home services and different skills. I've never called a plumber to solve an electrical problem. While I appreciate many a home remodeler that can do both, when it comes to calling in the right people, I trust those who have chosen their field, and I rely on their expertise for that reason.

Yes, we all are multitalented and possess a large collection of unique behaviors and skills that positively impact others. Your personal journey is to find out how your gifts differentiate you from everyone else. Your journey to capture what not to change will help you honor what to keep doing and will facilitate your success faster than guessing.

To stay in your unique lane doesn't sound hard unless you haven't figured out how to do that yet.

I have often witnessed how easily someone will ask another to step in for a fellow teammate, forgetting that the absent person has the unique skills to do the best job. In a time of need, we often just wish someone else could fill in. We seem to think everyone can wear all hats. We forget people are different enough to be specialized, and this is where teams often drift away from being as high performing as possible.

Whether working individually for a team or on a team, our individual talents and gifts are the things we do that naturally benefit the results we produce. People who are aware of working where they are "at their best" and embrace the idea of working in their "lane" know how to use their natural strengths, appreciate them, and can often solve problems faster by knowing where their work ends and another's begins. (I'm not talking about throwing your hands up and stating, "That's not my job." That's not effective or helpful—ever. I'm simply offering the description of how others perceive their relevance and know where the handoff is optimized for all talent to be included.)

You don't see Spider-Man always jumping in to drive Batman's car. OK, that may be a bad example since Spider-Man can totally get across town faster using his unique web-slinging abilities, but you get the point. These same people who understand what they do well often find themselves contributing on high-performing teams where each member understands each person's optimal contributions.

High-Performing Teams

High-performing teams know the specific talents on their teams, rarely overstep, and are known for their ability to outperform their competition, maintain higher employee retention rates, and create innovative approaches to problems. They are also recognized for the way they communicate with respect, utilize curiosity to lift ideas, and solve problems in ways that many teams never even attempt.

High-performing teams, however, don't always have the luxury to explore and discover one another's strengths before they jump into problem-solving mode. While they may each know their own, often they are learning about each other on the fly. Many of us who aspire to be similar in our higher-performance goals and problem-solving success must do the same. But how?

Good news. Whether working alone, reaching out for assistance while problem solving, or working on a team, you can still be creative in problem solving.

Like the diversity session with everyone looking at a setting of familiar objects and being asked to offer their thoughts, setting the context and providing a safe space to brainstorm needs to be communicated. Brainstorming needs all ideas to come forward without the threat of getting made fun of or being marginalized in any way.

This is a critical piece to getting a team to collaborate openly. I often remind managers and leaders that all employees need three basic things:

- safety (physical and psychological), which includes accepted ways to communicate;
- to be included—and know that all details they need will be provided and communicated;
- to be treated with dignity—in communications, treatment, and career growth.

These are the basics.

High-performing teams do the basics with ease and elevate their ability to connect using several more elements: curiosity to stay open to ideas, speaking positively to each other, and assessing what is going right—before change is implemented.[41]

Positive Language Works

In 2004 Losada and Heady published their study of positivity and connectivity in the *American Behavioral Scientist* publication. Their work shed light on how teams use positive statements to drive more engagement, pace, and results than their competitors. Losada and Heady found that high-performing teams use five positive statements for every one negative statement. And that was the average![42]

The data showed a 5.6 to 1 ratio. Compare this to moderately performing teams with a 1.8 positive to every negative, and poor performing teams performing far less. Ouch.

How did teams achieve this ratio? Losada and Heady offered that these teams would ask positively framed questions, based upon their understanding of the topic, and implement three important principles:

- Positive questions promote learning and engagement.
- Positive questions move thinking forward to shape the future.
- Positive questions inspire new energy and action.

At work, positive language sets individual contributors, high performers, and innovative teams apart. For those in leadership, it is an important factor that increases the retention of talented employees.

I didn't grow up in an environment full of positive statements. My childhood was marred by the unhappiness of my dad, who never really rebalanced after my mom died when I was a child. When people are unhappy, they often project their frustrations onto others, and it becomes exhausting to be the recipient of so much frustration. I was not used to hearing positive comments, having anyone be curious about my day, or being asked to contribute in a conversation. I was criticized often and told what to do, and my opinions were not asked or valued. Due to that, I started to hide from my own thoughts and concentrate on how to survive in such a negative environment. I became sensitive to how to react, instead of how to participate.

This way of reacting to my environment gradually became a habit. Habits are sneaky and key to pay attention to, because they limit what you stay curious about. Rarely do we seek out to learn something about what we already do. Instead we may seek out the new. For me, staying positive was a new concept, and becoming curious is not useful when you are in survival mode—I didn't realize how my survival habits were getting in the way of becoming who I wanted to be.

This concept of staying curious, speaking with the intention of staying positive, and asking what I did that mattered to others was so foreign when I started my research, I looked for ways to dismiss the evidence that this works.

Don't wait as long as I did to put this to work. Jump in and just try out a few conversations by providing the context and asking for one thing and an example.

Here are some examples of this concept for your own benefit, which can be edited for your team too.

Using the Positive Principles Topics

Positive questions promote learning and engagement.
Topic: client
- Ask,
  One **thing:** "What is the one thing you feel I/we do exceptionally well
  Context: that allows us to meet your needs?"
  Example: Then ask for an example.

Positive questions shape the future.
Topic: employee development
- Ask,

  Context: "We may have positions open in the future."
  One thing: "What role interests you most?"
  Example: "What are you doing now to prepare for that role?" or, "How we can help you get prepared?"

Positive questions inspire energy and action.
Topic: promotion options
- Ask,

  Context: "As our organization grows,
  One thing: what is the one area where you feel I am positioned for the best growth?"
  Example: "What do you feel are actions I could consider that will allow me to optimize that growth?"

Chapter 8 Questions

1. Whether on a team or leading a team, what is one benefit this ASK Framework would bring to team performance?
2. Identify the question you will ask your team member(s). The ASK Framework is meant to be used in private 1:1 scenarios. Goals don't happen without a timeline: What is your desired timeframe to ask your question with each member of your team?

Your Own Speed Bumps

Don't confuse life's speed bumps with stop signs.
—Anonymous

J ust like I experienced, old habits can get in the way of new ones. And developing consistent habits is a challenge. When I tried to implement new habits, it was amazing what got in the way. Then I realized we experience this in individual ways. When daylight saving time hits, or we decide to start going to the gym, or we take a different route to work, or we stop smoking, the struggle to change is exciting at first, then becomes hard as our old habits re-emerge.

Old-Habit Speed Bumps

Smokers attest to the harsh difficulties of quitting, especially if they used their smoke breaks to spend time with others as an excuse to take a walk outside or just to get away from their desk.

"Dad! I thought you quit!" I remember being so exasperated. I hated walking out of the house with my clothes smelling like we lived in a bar.

"Well, sweetie, turns out it calms my nerves, and I use it as a great excuse to step outside when I need a break at work. I just can't give that up right now."

I shook my head, disappointed. *What would it take?*

My dad eventually forgot he smoked when dementia hit later in his life—small silver linings from a disease that takes all closure away from loved ones. While I am a fierce nonsmoker, I do not condone wishing dementia on anyone for the sake of forgetting to smoke—it was just a very small blessing to not have to remind him not to smoke in a smoke-free facility.

Can You Replace an Old Habit?

To succeed at developing a new habit, simply replacing the old habit isn't the answer. A perspective shift prompts change to become more organic and meaningful. This is vital in helping people replace any habit with a better one. With the right insight or motivation, some people have quit smoking immediately—a death in the family, lung cancer of a fellow smoking friend—while others still struggle. It's the meanings we've associated with the habit that need to be addressed. It may feel as if I am picking on smokers, but I'm simply using the habit as an example of how hard it is to break a habit that brings some people joy, release, an escape, or an identity. These are all reasons to justify the habit.

It can be equally hard to change eating habits, sleeping habits, or even cussing. Things we have developed as habits served us well at some point in time. When the time comes to change those habits, however, we have built an entire support system around them without even realizing it. So how do you change this?

Habit Stacking

In *Atomic Habits*, author James Clear advocates habit stacking: developing new habits using micro steps.[43] In habit stacking, Clear proposes building a new habit by adding a small habit to your already-established habits. For example, it's been said that the hardest part of working out is getting ready and leaving your house to go to the gym. Once you're there, you end up doing the work due to the supportive environment of machines, classes, and other people to work out with. So how do you make it easier to get to the gym? Using Clear's micro-step idea, set out your workout clothes and everything you need to get out the door the night before. When you wake up, don't question yourself—put your gym clothes on and leave. Or if you intend to go to the gym on the way home from work, sign up for a class that makes you get there, without looking for a happy-hour excuse to derail your efforts. Take your pick.

Clear advocates for thoroughly thinking through how to be successful and breaking new habits into easy steps that help you feel successful. This method creates a higher success rate, especially in habits that have been established over time.[44] If you are used to getting up and having a cup of coffee every morning and you now need to put that coffee off until after your workout and you're on your way to work, find a special coffeehouse you can visit to make it more fun. This doesn't mean that some mornings when you cannot get to the gym you don't have coffee—it's just a new schedule on days you work out.

When we build in small steps of success that are also fun, we receive mental and physical rewards from successfully accomplishing one step with a new habit while not having to completely let go of the old. When you step out of your old habits one step at a time, you are on your way to introducing anything you want into your life. It is you taking small risks that feel attainable.

> You only make impact when you take risks.
> —Shenae Grimes

New-Habit Speed Bumps

Adding a new habit on top of established ones can be as hard as starting a new habit where you've previously had none. Creating space for a new habit can feel like wedging in an unwelcome chore. We must address this because old habits will always win out unless we are mindful and plan with purpose.

"I miss the gym," my lovely assistant offered while on a video call recently. "I just don't get motivated in my own living room with the video on the TV. I end up quitting after thirty minutes. If I were in class, I'd never give up."

She laughed. "And I'm an introvert!"

She sighed. "I can't imagine what others are going through."

She sounded defeated. The 2020 quarantine adaptations of her favorite workouts simply weren't working for her. They weren't working for a lot of people forced to work from home, homeschool kids, and juggle the demands of work on top of staying safe and healthy.

Like her trying to adapt her workout to a different environment, nearly everyone worldwide was being asked to adapt some aspect of their life to compensate for the health measures needed to reduce the widespread risks associated with the new virus. Some much more than others.

Asking you to implement this new ASK Framework and gather information on what you do right is also an adaptation. We will all encounter speed bumps on our road to successfully working in this new technique into desired conversations. Either about work or anywhere else. Like any new habit, though, it is worth the effort and the information you gain.

Mindset Speed Bumps

Every athlete knows that practice works. Yet they will tell you it is also one of the hardest parts of the sport. Why?

It's repetitive and redundant. It's more mental work to keep going to practice than the physical.[45] In practice, you make mistakes, you must regroup to improve, and you must talk to yourself to keep doing it when it's hard. However, through practice, you will improve. And as we've witnessed with great athletes like Michael Jordan and many others, practice will become a great habit that will set you apart from others.[46]

Practice sets you apart. This is why we practice having conversations to discover what others appreciate, love, admire, or gain by working with us. By setting out to discover the one thing you don't need to change, you gain information that will surprise you, will build your confidence in this method, and will help you to impact your career growth. You'll develop finesse in handling conversations and will even improve how you step into the tougher conversations.

I recommend practicing with people who know you well and want your best efforts rewarded. Practice with people whom you can safely make mistakes with. And if you can, choose people who have a sense of humor. This is a valuable bonus.

Here are some examples to practice with:

Context: "When we go out to social events,
One thing: what's one thing you enjoy the most about going together?"
Example: "Can you give me an example of the most recent time that has happened?"

Context: "When we go to family events,
One thing: what is one thing that shows you that I'm having a great time?"
Example: "Can you give me an example of when you've seen that before?"

Context: "When you need help,
One thing: what's the one thing I do that helps you feel supported?"
Example: "Can you give me an example of when that has happened?"

Context: "When it comes to gift giving,
One thing: what is the one thing I can do to make it easier for you?"
Example: "Can you give me an example of how that would look like to you?"

Context: "When we talk on the phone,

One thing: what is the one thing I've said that surprises you in a good way?"
Example: "Can you share with me when that happened?"

I started with my husband and then asked questions of my daughter and son, only to be surprised at their answers. I quickly realized that I didn't have an accurate idea of how they saw me. Living proof of misaligned self-awareness.

I'm not sure what I imagined I'd hear, but I learned things I hadn't thought they paid attention to. The examples included the following:

"Mom, you amazed me at how you could pick up and organize a move with what the military threw at us."

"I've just now realized that you managed to have your own business in five different moves, and I can't imagine how you did that."

"I'm continually amazed at all you did when I was falling apart and mad at you and dad for another move."

"And the way you had to deal with Grandpa in his last ten years of life while your brother was called up to deploy five different times."

Since my own family had surprised me, I wondered what information I would gain from my colleagues, clients, and community. I couldn't wait to approach people who could provide insights that might help build my success.

If I hadn't taken the first brave step and practiced with my family, I might never have had this unique insight for myself, and now my clients as well.

So let's do the same at work. Here are some examples of questions I've asked and heard others ask as well.

A team member:
Context: "The last time we worked together, we were both participating on a team project."

One thing: "What was one thing you felt I did well that contributed to the end results?"
Example: "Could you give me an example of how you recognize that?"

From a meeting together:
Context: "The meeting yesterday seemed to go great!"
One thing: "Who did you feel contributed the most to it going so well?"
Example: "Can you give me an example of when you saw that in action?"

With a supervisor:
Context: "I'd really love to understand more about growth opportunities in our organization."
One thing: "Can you share with me where you see the next opportunities are emerging?"
Example: "Can you share with me what that timeline may look like for someone in my position?"

Client meeting:
Context: "Yesterday, when we were both on the virtual conference meeting and I was presenting,
One thing: what one piece of information did you feel was most valuable to the client?"
Example: "Can you give me an example of how you recognized that?"

Project member:
Context: "Whenever we get to work together on a project,
One thing: what is one thing you know you can count on me to contribute?"
Example: "Can you give me an example of how you see that?"

With these examples, my goal is that you start developing your own questions within the ASK Framework based upon what you want to know about your own work performance, growth opportunities, or even how the team wants to continue working virtually or in person.

Be mindful—don't let your doubts get in your way. Planning will always help. And yes, you will forget certain steps, so practicing will help you connect with the parts that provide the most meaning for you.

Here are the speed bumps to watch out for:

Doubts
- Doubting the value of this information
- Doubting the value of obtaining "the one thing"

Planning
- Lack of planning what to ask
  - Lack of planning whom to ask

Forgetting
- Forgetting to provide context
- Forgetting to ask for an example
- Forgetting to stay within the context; falling back into the habit of asking what to improve

In these instances, you are the only thing holding back your success. Therefore, I'm asking you to jump into this new adventure to create these new habits so you can fully be

- thinking about your success,
- controlling your own growth,
- interacting with people who have influence over your success, and
  - stepping into conversations.

This will show you how much you want success and how much you want to stop sitting back and waiting to see what other people will do for you.

Stop waiting for other people to move you forward.

If you never ask, people will assume you don't want help

By asking what you do right, you immediately send the message that you are ready for people to help you become successful.

The Doubt Speed Bump

Many people doubt the value of new information. Any time we try something new, we find it inconvenient, and we wonder if we should continue.

Asking other people what you do that they appreciate feels new, weird, and awkward. For some, it may even seem prideful or self-seeking. Seeking information that reveals someone else's perspective is not selfish. It allows them to feel valued.[47] The act of asking can be a gift to the other person just as much as the information is a gift to you.

We are consistently looking for ways to become more successful. We are meant to learn. However, the quest to learn more all the time takes a toll when we are always second-guessing what we do that matters in the first place. In contrast, when we have good information, we feel safe in offering our talents and skills to others. Then when we are ready to grow, we seek information that builds upon what we already do well. Only when we are building upon good talent can we reach higher.

> We can't solve problems using the same kind of thinking we used when we created them.
> —Albert Einstein

We are starting to see how our incessant desire to be better, faster, and stronger—while living longer—is taking a toll on our physical and mental health. It's no wonder we could sabotage our own success by doubting the value of implementing a new idea. If it were important, wouldn't someone else already have invented it and told us about it?

I'm glad Jeff Bezos didn't think that way.[48] If he had, we never would have experienced the thrill of having a last-minute birthday gift delivered to us via Amazon in a location nowhere near a store.

Or toilet paper when the stores were vacant of any while we all prepared to clean and sanitize while housing our entire family at home for long periods of time at the beginning of the COVID-19 pandemic of 2020.

Just as we have witnessed the confusion at the onset of the pandemic of 2020, planning will be your secret weapon.

The Planning Speed Bump

You do need to plan, even just a little. Why is planning important? It helps you gain confidence. When you plan these new conversations, make a list of people you feel would support your success.

Have a practice list and a career list. The practice list includes your family and friends, people you feel confident around, and those who would allow you to practice and mess up. The career list includes people you've had in your professional life and those who have true influence over your current and future career success.

These lists are important because they help you see your circles of influence.

Your practice list includes friends and family. There are some added benefits in this. Your confidence may also increase as you list friends and family you can laugh with while practicing. You will look forward to goofing off together and explaining what you are trying to accomplish. Often when people practice with friends, the friends start implementing it too. When your friends grow in their ability to do this, everyone wins. Talk about fun incentive!

Your career list includes people you work with as peers, coworkers, direct reports, mentors, and even clients. If you have a noticeably short career list, ask yourself why. Have you selected only the people you like? Do you doubt the value of some coworkers' perspectives? I challenge you to reflect on this and remember that you might gain valuable insight from others' opinions, even if you think they might not give you a positive response. I'm not asking you to practice with people who seek to make you uncomfortable or who genuinely do not give you good vibes. I just want you to think hard about why your lists look the way they do.

After your practice and career lists, make a list of people you'd like to ask but are scared to. This will be your someday list. As you gain practice and confidence, please consider asking people from your someday list. This someday list may include people who may not have had the best experience with you, former bosses whom you truly don't know how they feel about you, or a potential employer whom you only know through a referral or in passing but with whom you would love to work. This planning is a growth exercise and gives you a unique opportunity to learn more about yourself as well as the people you admire.

Planning is simple. All it requires is that you make lists and imagine when you can connect with the people on the list. You can do this! Now make at least one coffee date or phone call to try.

> Speedbumps never stop a car; they just provide a good reminder of what to get over.

The Forgetting Speed Bumps

We forget how to execute these conversations effectively when we haven't practiced or when we hit unexpected speed bumps. Sometimes we forget to incorporate all three steps. We may get excited about the one thing and forget the context, or we may get excited about learning about the one thing and forget to ask for an example. Whenever we forget, we regroup and continue to ask, using the three elements of context, one thing, and an example in different orders when needed.

Because . . .

- You need the context for clarity.
- You need to limit the information to one thing to maximize the information given.
- You need the example so you can gain perspective.

Shake It Up

To manage our forgetfulness, practice asking in different ways. For example, practice switching the order of the context, one thing, and example. This is a framework, not a strict formula; shake it up a little.

Try this: "I'd love to know one thing I'm doing right. Specifically, I'd love for you to share an example of one thing I'm doing right in our weekly stand-up meetings."

Or this: "I'd love for you to share an example, from your perspective, of one thing I did right when we worked together for our last client."

Practicing in a way that feels comfortable and fun will increase your chances of remembering the need for context to help the other person be successful, one thing to help your brain get a great piece of information, and an example so you can see yourself from their perspective.

Have fun with it! The more fun you have with this exercise, the more endorphins you release, and the more you will succeed in being consistent in the conversations.

Action may not always bring happiness, but there is no happiness without action.
—Benjamin Disraeli

Chapter 9 Experiments

1. Success is achieved by *doing*: Set your timer for five minutes, and write your list of family and friends who you will practice the ASK Framework.

2. It never hurts to write your practice questions down for each person, then commit to asking five family and friends in the next forty-eight hours. *Just do it* (thank you, Nike!).

The People Speed Bumps

S peed bumps can be people too. These are often people you anticipate being a challenge.

However, there are those you don't see getting in your way—and they are the ones we least expect: the unexpected speed bumps. These may be people who fear the results of your change. They might fear anything new, or maybe they fear their world changing because of your success or growth. These unexpected speed bumps may be the friends, family, or coworkers you interact with most.

When my clients hit an unexpected speed bump, it's normally from someone they assumed would provide a positive conversation. When the person acts unexpectedly negatively, that is the surprise we get to work through. While it does provide a new twist for the client, I do see this more often than even I expect.

When this happens, it is good practice to be mindful and understand that a person's negative reaction may have nothing to do with you. Most of the time it's due to their own fear of change. If they see you becoming motivated to learn about your own success, they may doubt their own success. If you don't include them in your practice questions, they won't know what you are implementing, and they'll feel excluded. If you are having more fun than before, they may become envious and want the same fun. New things can trigger insecurities in others, and you might not see it coming.

Take the time to ask what is bothering them. If they share, great. It may offer an opportunity to grow together. Include them in what you are doing, and laugh together about how awkward or weird it may feel. Share. Help them form a list of people they could ask to gain the same information about themselves. Support them in understanding one thing they do right. Get excited about doing this together, and share the good news with each other. If you tackle this exercise along with a friend, you have accountability. Supporting each other in practice means you can support each other in success too.

However, if a person you've approached does not have anything positive to offer or insists on marginalizing your efforts to have an exploratory conversation using the ASK formula, this may be a red flag of someone who is struggling in their own life. Again, do not take someone else's negativity personally. This is just not the right person or the right time to include them in your efforts to gather positive information.

You need to associate with people that inspire you, people that challenge you to rise higher, people that make you better. Don't waste your valuable time with people that are not adding to your growth. Your destiny is too important.
—Joel Osteen

We Have Control

Remember, when we frame the context in a positive way, the information we receive usually stays positive.[49] If the context is not provided, the other person feels they have license to give you their opinion, and that could be negative.[50]

When I ask for information, my intent is not to give someone license to be negative. If you do not provide context, that's exactly what some people will do. I have known people to feel that, when you ask them for information, they are given freedom to provide it, positive or negative. If you provide no context, you give them permission to imagine there is a problem to solve or that you are open to whatever they have to say. Often it may be negative, simply due to their desire to feel helpful.

Context and clarity are key to lifting one another up. Clearly defined context keeps the door securely closed to negative input or output.

The biggest emotion in creation is the bridge to Optimism.
—Brian May

Meet Nelly and Charlie

Keeping the door closed to negativity requires well-defined context. This provides clarity and will help you maintain a positive conversation. However, we must discuss what happens when the other person doesn't operate within that context.

We'll cheerfully call these folks "Negative Nelly" and "Constructive-Criticism Charlie."

Nelly and Charlie represent people who are unaccustomed to the idea of finding out what anyone does right. They ignore the positive slant of your question and dive into trying to help you improve.

Stop them kindly. Here's what I mean. I met Nelly in the hallway and asked her about a presentation I had done recently. I was quick to let her know I wanted one thing that went well.

Nelly looked confused.

"Nelly, I think you are one of the best people to ask this because you see me present these reports all the time. So I wanted to just start with the last time we were in a meeting together" (context). What is the best part of my report presentations?"

Nelly paused. "You know, I need to think about that—you do a lot of things well that I just haven't put much thought to it, but I did notice something I know would help."

I quickly put my hand up—gently.

"Nelly, whoa! I love that you're ready to jump in to help me grow." I laughed. "Today, however, I need to focus on what not to change before I go a changing again." I could feel the cheesy "don't go changing" song lyrics floating in my head.

"Well," she said, "let me think about it and get back with you."

I happily thanked her and moved on down the hall.

The next day I ran into Charlie.

"Charlie, you and I were working on a project together last year."

He acknowledged he remembered.

"What was the most effective thing I contributed to that project to you?"

He took a moment and confessed he'd have to think about it.

"Ya know, though, I do have some constructive criticism to share on how things started."

Again, I smiled and put my hand up.

"Charlie, thanks for letting me know you have that handy. I'm currently gathering what I do well first, but when I'm ready to learn more, can I come find you on that?"

"Oh, of course. Happy to help!" he eagerly offered.

And I moved on. Teaching Charlie about my quest could wait for another day. Not everyone is ready for your new approach. Don't take it personally—they just see themselves being helpful in different ways.

Remember, when you smile or laugh, you show your lightness, and it's perfectly OK to say that you can't work on correcting something today. You need to understand what you do right today before you start correcting anything tomorrow. Set the example on this, and it will turn heads in a good way.

Anytime you stop people from offering improvement or constructive-criticism insights, this may surprise them, so say it kindly and give them a moment to consider your words. Your kindness will pay off, even if they can't think of anything to offer.

Let them know that when they do have something to say, you'll be grateful and open to listening. Then let it go. Usually this person will eventually give you a wonderful nugget. Even if they don't, you've had the unique opportunity of seeing things from their perspective. This is a huge win for both of you.

> Patience is not simply the ability to wait—it's how we behave while we're waiting.
> —Joyce Meyer

When Nelly and Charlie Don't Get It

Let's say that no matter how kind you are, Nelly and Charlie can't find any value in telling you what you do right. They see the world through a lens of problem solving, and they're moving down that same road in your conversation. The way to handle this is with patience, consistency, and kindness.

Explain that people need to know what is going right before they start changing more than they need to. (You can cite the popular saying "If it isn't broke, don't fix it.") Then immediately ask for an example of what you do right. You've already given context and asked for one thing, so jump to the example now. They may give you a positive example, even if they don't recognize the value of this process.

Tell them you'd like to come back later to find out what they think you can improve upon, when you're ready to hear it. Normally, they feel complimented that you value their insights enough to want more later. This works with people who tend to be negative. Everyone wants to feel valued, regardless of temperament.

> Knowing trees, I understand the meaning of patience. Knowing grass, I can appreciate persistence.
> —Hal Borland

Meet Taylor and Stewart

There are unhappy people at work who never enjoy other people's successes. These people are often toxic in their approach to others, regardless of the topic or event. We've all met one or two in our time.

When people are negative, spiteful, or toxic in general, they usually have an unmet personal need. You may never learn what that is, and it might not be related to work. People's personal lives often infiltrate the way they handle themselves at work. So while you may have no control over how to make the toxic person happy or help them get their needs met, you could still benefit from learning how they see you at work.

While I don't recommend starting with negative or toxic individuals on your journey to find out what you do right, you may run into them anyway. Their perspective could still be valuable to you.

Meet Stewart

Stewart was having a bad day: Generally, Stewart is steady in work efforts and managerial style. Unfortunately, she is currently going through a tough divorce and has a special-needs child who requires exhaustive medical attention. She is constantly sleep deprived or stressed about money, and this negatively affects how she sees things at work.

"Hey, Stewart, I'm hoping to gain some information from you about that last report I turned in to you."

"Oh, sure." Stewart seemed distracted.

"I'm hoping to gain what was the most helpful aspect of that report for you."

Stewart looked at me blankly.

"I'm not sure I can remember much about that report. Sorry. What did you need to know again?"

"Stewart, are you OK?" I asked

Tears welled up, and she was trying hard to keep them back.

"Can I hug you?" I offered.

She quickly nodded as tears escaped, and we just hugged. Now was not the time to ask about me.

Later that day I ran into Taylor as he was getting ready to leave. Taylor was also part of building the report that had gotten turned in to Stewart and was managing a project I was helping with now. And while Taylor possessed perspective with more recent experience of working with me, I was leery of him even on a good day.

Recently at a board meeting, Taylor was asked about something that had gone wrong with reporting new data. Taylor threw the entire team under the bus, yet he was happy to take all the credit when the department's budget came in under projected expenses. His negative behavior was reliable, regardless of the circumstances, and we often referred to him as Toxic Taylor. I doubted Taylor would want to offer anything good. But I jumped in anyway because I knew it would be unbelievably valuable to understand how he viewed me on a professional level.

"Hi, Taylor. It looks like you are on your way out. Can I have a quick five minutes?"

"Sure, but just five." He was gathering his things.

"I'm looking for an example of my best contribution when we were collaborating on the report we turned in to Stewart. If you need to think it over, that's totally fine. I just wanted to plant the question in your head to gain that information when you have the chance," I said calmly.

His head turned to me. "What's the reason?"

"I'm gathering info on what contributions I offer that work for others so I can keep doing them. I'm trying to raise my self-awareness of what truly helps others in case it's different than what I think."

The look on Taylor's face was priceless, as if this idea were so foreign, he might think I was crazy. I waited.

"I'll think on it. Let me get back to you."

"Thanks." I waved as he left.

I did hear back from Taylor a month later. He sauntered into my office and let me know that my due diligence on gathering the intel needed for the report was what impressed him the most. It might have taken a while, but that insight was priceless to me because I was not normally the person who took care of that information. Score!

Include Them

If you're dealing with a Steady Stewart who's simply going through a difficult time, show compassion and let them know you realize they're having a rough day. Set up a time to come back and ask your question. You can always let them know the context. This will give them the chance to think. By recognizing their current state, you also let them know they are valued, their time is valued, and their perspective is worth the wait.

If your manager is Toxic Taylor, know that your value is worth the asking price. First practice asking others and collect information about what you already do well. If you then ask your manager the same question, you will be able to understand how much value to place on their viewpoint too.

That said, if the manager's viewpoint is the one that will affect your next promotion, ask your question carefully: "Taylor, since you're my manager, I value your perspective on my performance. I want to gain insight into what you think I do right so that when you need me to improve, I'll know what not to mess with. Is now a good time to ask you a question about that, or can I grab a few moments later?"

Whether it's now or later, remember the following:

- **Context:** "Taylor, I'm interested in how you view my performance in presenting information during our team meetings."
- **One thing:** "Can you tell me one thing I do well when presenting information each week?"
- **Example:** "Thanks for that. Can you give me an example of when I've done it better than other times?"

- **Acknowledgment:** "I appreciate your time. Thanks for the information."

Then thank Taylor and walk away with a wave.

Let everything you say be good and helpful, so that your words
will be an encouragement to those who hear them.
Ephesians 4:29

Chapter 10 Questions

1. Who is the Negative Nelly or Criticism Charlie in your professional or personal life?
2. What question can you ask to gain valuable and reframed insights and examples from that person? This may be a great piece of information to add to your Superhero File (or you may discover there isn't, and that's important to know too.)

Verbal Speed Bumps

The most ineffective thing that can happen in an information-gathering conversation is hearing all that we "should" have done. Take the word "should" as a red flag. When you practice conversations to gain positive information and hear a "should," it unexpectedly defeats the purpose. It can change your positive conversation into a lasting, negative experience.

Toxic Talk

The *Oxford English Dictionary* (2018) defines "should" as a verb "used to indicate obligation, duty, or correctness, typically when criticizing someone's actions."[51] Research done by DeAnna Murphy has revealed that "should" offers more about the provider of this word than the receiver. For example, when *we* say someone "should" have done something, that is, "she should have finished her work," it often simply means *we* wish she had done her work.[52]

Criticism is not what we are after. As we've proven, it's not an effective way to teach or learn. Criticism is the gateway for unhealthy expectations of ourselves and others and can lead to toxic relationships, internally and externally. Unfortunately, the word "should" often reveals that the conversation is heading into a place of frustration instead of productivity.

Toxic Shoulds

DeAnna Murphy, of People Acuity, introduced me to the battle of the shoulds. This was such a lightbulb moment for me as a self-criticizing, well-meaning mom, plus an overachieving manager and director, that I now include this in all my coaching. She is brilliant on coaching this topic to avoid toxic teams, and here is what I learned.

Any conversation that has a should in it is one to be wary of.

Why? Because the word "should" masks frustration—the person (who could be us) just hasn't gone far enough in thinking to identify exactly what it is that is frustrating.[53]

Let's unpack the following common examples:

- I should
- You should
- They should

We fall into the "I should" trap when we badger ourselves about anything, when we think we should be able to do something on our own but we can't (which is akin to self-shaming). We fall in the "you should" trap when we project our goals onto someone else without considering what they want to do. This puts others on the defensive. Or we use "they should" to give our opinions about others in a nonhelpful, nonloving manner. All three of these "should" are toxic triggers. While they mask frustration instead of calming a frustration, they cause more devastation.

I should

"I should" critically and quickly leads us down the path to internal toxic stress. Our desires, expectations, or aspirational standards cause this internal pressure. This often leads to worry.

Worry is a waste of the imagination.
—Walt Disney

This internal toxic stress is different from the positive stress that comes from challenging ourselves to meet a positive, realistic goal.

Positive stress fuels us.

Toxic stress destabilizes us.

You know when it's there. It gives you a headache, upsets your stomach, and invites its sidekick worry to come in and make itself comfortable. How do we avoid it?

When we say to ourselves "I should," Murphy offers that we become independent. We self-judge and self-shame ourselves into thinking we should be able to do something on our own. This is where our ego can get the best of us. When we seek a solution independently, we shut out other people who may have a better solution.

This sudden withdrawal into "I should" thinking creates a win-lose scenario with you. You may provide the solution (win), but you may not know if there was a better way to get there because you were determined to do it by yourself (lose). This type of thinking convinces your brain that you don't need others' help, even though others might have a better idea.

When you start thinking *I should be able to do this on my own* or *I should write the report by myself* or *I should finish this project on my own because everyone else is too busy*, that is when you pull away and isolate yourself. Working in a vacuum has a lot of pitfalls.

Here is where you can brilliantly show up for yourself with the ASK Framework.

I'm aware that many professionals (like accountants, engineers, and data coders) require isolated focus, and certain personality types (like introverts) thrive on time alone. However, when others will benefit from the outcome of your work, it's worth seeking the thoughts and opinions of others. You don't know what you don't know. Others may expect an aspect of work you may not have considered. This is where asking for the "one thing" helps to clarify expectations. That way when you work alone you're not alone in understanding the outcome, and you don't get misled by the "I shoulds."

"I should" is the fastest way to find a pitfall.

Context: "I think I can do this on my own, yet I realize you have a stake in the outcome."

One thing: "What is the most important aspect of this project's outcome that you'd like me to stay aware of?"
Example: "Can you give me an example of how that might look like from your perspective?"

You Should

Chris rushed in. "Sorry I'm late. I'm just struggling with the new road closures. I can't wait until they figure this thing out."

"This is the third day in a row. Don't you think you should leave earlier?" Shane said in frustration.

Chris stopped short. She had three kids she had to get off to school as a single mom.

"I can't make the bus come earlier, Shane—I would if I could."

The tensions rose before the day even had started.

This is the beginning of a toxic interaction simply because questions for clarity weren't offered before a should showed up. When a should shows up, people feel judged, shamed, criticized, and selfish.

"You should" makes people defensive.

When someone tells you "you should," Murphy offers that we tend to feel judged and get defensive.[54]

We forget to realize that the other person is imposing their limited view on us without knowing the full picture of the circumstances.

When you feel the desire to correct or defend yourself, remember that this is a defensive response to the other person's lack of information. Don't slip into a victim attitude thinking how wrongly you were treated. This leads to toxic thoughts and actions. The negative impact can be widespread.

The best way to turn something toxic into something productive is to refuse to take it personally. Realize that the other person doesn't have all the information. If this person is a coworker, manager, or supervisor, you may need to correct their misconception. For your success at work, make an appointment to sit down with this person and share the information you were working from so you can clear up any misunderstandings. For example:

Context: "Recently, you made a comment where you felt I should have done something differently."
One thing: "I understand how I may have frustrated you, so what one piece of information can I provide you to have a better conversation?"
Example: "If after that you still feel I should have acted differently, I'd love for you share an example of how I could do that in the future."

They Should

This is the typical baseline for all gossip.

When you say things like,

"They should do better reporting,"

"They should take time to care about their employees,"

"They should do a better job on payroll,"

"They should pay attention to the workload," or

"They should not expect us to work overtime,"

you are voicing a frustration and projecting that frustration on a group. This means you are offering your opinion. If your opinion is not based on all the facts, it tends to get viewed as starting gossip.

You may think you are bonding over a common grievance, but it's likely you are spreading information that isn't entirely correct. And when it is someone else's opinion that is being shared, it's gossip.

"They should" is the fastest way to start gossip.

It's dangerous to discuss something about someone with another coworker just so the two of you can build a stronger connection. This can quickly become toxic because you disconnect from the person you are discussing. You're using a discussion about another to bond with the person you are talking to. This never works in the long run and will likely backfire. That coworker will realize you may do the same toward them. You've created multiple toxic external stressors with one conversation.

When you knowingly engage in spreading information in this manner, it is gossip. Gossip is negative. Compliments are positive. Be aware of this because when someone else turns the conversation negative, saying, "he/she/they should," you need to redeem the situation by concentrating on what people do right. For example:

> **Context:** "I realize you are frustrated, and it seems that Harry has something to do with that."
> **One thing:** "But what is the one thing Harry does well that helps you?"
> **Example:** "Can you give me an example of what it looks like when Harry does that well?"
> **Thanks:** "Thanks for sharing. We all mess up sometimes, and it's good to be reminded about what Harry does well to help you."

If you don't like something, change it. If you can't change it, change your attitude.
—Maya Angelou

Will this make you unique? Yes. Will negative people stop approaching you to gossip? Likely. Is that a bad thing? Absolutely not. People will start to realize you have their back when others talk negatively, and they will rely on you to be that voice of reason among the group. Changing the conversation in this way puts you in a trusted and valuable position.

Things You Can't Change

Some elements of your life may not be in your control all the time. However, what you do about your own mental state is entirely in your control all the time.

> If you don't like something, change it. If you can't change it,
> change your attitude.
> —Maya Angelou

Choose wisely how you look at every situation. Understand what is in your control and what is not. I often must remind myself that internal toxic stress is a choice. If I am worrying, then I am likely choosing to take on things that are not in my control. The things that are in my control are the things I can affect with my own action. Action works to neutralize the stress I impose on myself as I move toward accomplishing what I can attain. You choose what you can change, based on your own behavior. Then choose to stay in that boundary of what you can change.

Change is in
the Choice.
—Jim Rohn

Chapter 11 Questions

1. Write an example of when you experienced one of the "shoulds": I should, you should, they should.
2. What was the point of frustration that prompted the "should"? If you don't know, it's because it is hard to know when someone projects their frustration onto you.
3. Now that you know more about how a frustration tends to prompt the "shoulds," think back to an "I should" and unpack what you were really frustrated by at that moment. What was that frustration?

Recap & Rewards

Try the ASK Framework. It is a rewarding experience. To make it effective, understand that insight will come gradually. When you collect the one thing others credit you for doing—from multiple people in all the areas of your work and life—you will collect priceless insights into your own unique character.

Remember the Basics

In the training and development world, repetitive practice is designed to enhance your brain and the way you think and act. This is often called *cognitive loading*, a term that means "learning in stages." Layering experiences that load onto the other to solidify the practice of finding out all that you currently do well lends the practice to become habit. Thus, you become great at collecting things that reveal your own unique gifts and talents. You won't learn everything you are doing right in one day, with one person, or with just one question. This knowledge will build. You will learn in stages. Cognitive loading at its best.

It's easy to open your mouth and ask a new question, but there's more to this process for creating lasting and effective change. Thinking about it, preparing for it, and receiving it is an easy idea. It takes intention.

> It is not good enough for things to be planned—they still have to be done; for the intention to become a reality, energy has to be launched into operation.
> —Walt Kelly

Be Clear about the Context

If you are laser focused on what you'd like to know, you'll be more likely to get it. Be focused about the topic you're using to set the context. This could be your work in an industry, or it could be something specific, like a skill, such as presentation skills from a recent meeting, report formatting for a client, team communications frameworks, a team-building activity, or your own personal communication skills.

Letting the other person know exactly what you are interested in saves them from guessing or making a broad, sweeping statement that is too vague to be useful. It also saves you from the unexpected response from a contrasting scenario you are not prepared to unpack. Presenting the context drives specific and helpful information that can be applied to the specific situation. This type of clarity allows for an easier exchange of information. It also sets the other person up for success in giving you the information you can use.

Remember the earlier invitation to make a coffee date with someone? This is just a kind reminder to also include a variety of people. Decide whose insights you'd appreciate. Establish the context of the conversation, and when you get to connect, be willing to jump in with this new framework and approach.

Context example: "I'd like to get your insights from our meeting on Thursday, and how I presented to the group." (Notice the focus of the topic.)

One thing: "When I presented to the team, what *one thing* did I do that had a positive impact and that I could continue to do in the future?" Then wait for the answer.

Note: If they begin to add more than one thing, don't be afraid to stop them. Don't let them move on to a second topic. Remember, your brain needs to play around with just one thing to incorporate the new information with the right energy. Say, "Before you add to that answer, let me concentrate on the one thing you've already said. I'm happy to come back when I'm ready to process more."

The example: Often we forget to go for the best part. I encourage you to ask for an example of how they experienced it, or how they saw it, or what went right. This allows them to share information from their own perceptions and viewpoint. It is a priceless piece of insight, as you now get to see how they perceive your actions and work.

Simply state: "Thank you for sharing that information with me. I'd like to understand more. Can you share an example of how you recognized the impact?"

Welcome to Discovering YOU

Gaining a collection of the one thing you don't have to change in the many areas of your life is an amazing adventure. It will help you understand your value to your employer. This will contribute to your satisfaction and confidence right away and will help when you're interviewing or applying for a coveted promotion at work. It will help you see how your family values you and how your friends view you. It could even explain why those people interact with you the way they do.

Early in this book, I introduced the self-improvement trap (chapter 2). Are you ready to move past the trap? With the ASK Framework, you can!

By simply asking for information in a specific format, you can gain amazing knowledge about yourself. Here's what I want to know:

Will you do it?

How soon can you start?

Whom will you ask first?

It's an amazing way to solve the self-doubt, second-guessing, and low confidence problems that lead us to the self-improvement trap.

Tune your ears to wisdom and concentrate on understanding.

Proverbs 2:2

The Rewards Are Endless!

Every time I ask how often someone wants a piece of this positive goodness, the resounding response I get is "Always!"

When I ask how often people use the ASK Framework to gain that information, they answer with an uncomfortable shuffle, a sheepish grin, and a slight shrug.

"When it came down to it, I felt awkward. I need to practice this."

I never get upset, because incorporating any new idea into action is hard. The challenge is not "Can you do it?" but rather "Will you keep trying to do it?" You will answer "Yes" only when the greater purpose of why you need to do it resonates with your own needs.

Here are the BIG reasons why focusing on the positive is beneficial. You will

- increase your self-awareness of how others perceive your efforts and interpret your work;
- hear and understand how others communicate positive information;
- increase your confidence in the value of your contributions.

The added benefits that may surprise you.

- Learn who sees a larger view of your work, strengths, and talents, versus who sees only a little view.
- Gain trust in those who want to support your success, growth, and career direction.
- Improve your critical thinking around how others perceive success.
- Practice asking for, and receiving, information so you know how to deliver positive feedback effectively when asked by others.
- Connect with and understand how you can support your coworkers.
- Apply these same lessons to your personal life.

But Wait! There's More!

If you recognize that phrase from your favorite late-night shopping channel, it's to remind you that there are added benefits to be had! While this has been covered in earlier sections, I cannot stress enough the benefit of helping other people feel heard when you ask them for their insights.

To make it as meaningful as possible, I highly recommend connecting in person, which includes the added new benefit of video calls and facetime calls. Yes, phone calls work too.

I do not recommend having this conversation via email or text message. Neither party can detect tone or the other nuances that make conversations multi-dimensional and more meaningful.

Consider these rewards for the person who gives you positive feedback:

- They know you appreciate their perspective of success.
- They feel valued for their input and observations.

It's not just the person who gives feedback who is rewarded. Both of you connect on your path to success and build a relationship for networking down the road.

When Does This Count? Always!

To increase self-awareness and learn how others perceive your efforts and interpret your work, don't think it doesn't count in everything you do. My first experience of how valuable this approach is occurred when I was six years old.

Age Six

As I embraced the ASK Framework myself, I wanted to know if I had ever experienced this in my own life. My first memory of something similar came to mind as I recalled the loss of my mom. I discovered why I found this approach so meaningful. Here's my memory.

I was six years old, standing in the grass. The sun beat down from a gorgeous blue-sky June day in 1969 on a dirt farm road. I had been the only person able to climb out of the car wreckage, and I was now numbly standing on the side of the road as the emergency personnel worked feverishly to recover anyone else.

"Carole, thank you for being so brave," the nurse said, standing over me.

I looked up at her, shading my eyes, too much in shock to feel anything.

"When you asked where your brother was, I thought you meant he was somewhere else," she started. "But when you described that he had been in the car with you, I became worried. Because of you, we found your brother underneath the backseat bench. I think he's going to be OK."

The ride in the ambulance with him covered in blood is still etched in my memory. The memory fades in and out of that ambulance ride because I only looked back once to see if he was still there on the stretcher. I'm not sure any six-year-old knows to feel good when bad things happen. I surely didn't feel like a hero that day. It was too full of scary sadness and unknowns. I just remember being horribly scared at all the blood.

It got better—he cleaned up surprisingly good for a feisty three-year-old with a concussion and a broken jaw. And yes, there is more to this story. That day we both lost our mom and our grandparents. What I saw and what I can recite in detail haunted me for a long time. Until I looked back and started to understand who I am today from that one day.

That day was the first time I can remember that someone used this approach for me to witness the positive effect it would have on my confidence down the road. That nurse offered the context, the one thing I did right, and an example of the outcome. I had been the only person to wake up in a car that had rolled down a hill. We had been hit by a young drunk driver racing his friend on a motorcycle. When the car came to a stop, I awoke and climbed out the back window as the car lay smoking on its side. As the ambulance and neighbors rushed to help, I sat on the side of the road. It wasn't until I recalled my brother sitting next to me that I asked someone where he was.

I was six years old—no one had to listen to me. No one did at first. I could have just sat down and done nothing. And for some reason, I kept asking. I was persistent. I was determined. Until someone took me seriously. Looking back, I understand why I always feel compelled to speak up for others who may not be heard or push their voice. From one horrible day that took my mother and both her parents, my brother lived to retire as a successful marine who served twenty years with five deployments and is the father of two great young men. And I continue to speak up for voices that need to be heard to this day.

Why Be Motivated to Do This?

I wish I could remember that nurse's name. I know she wasn't consciously following a framework when she spoke to me. She was being kind enough to let me know what I did and the result of my speaking up. I wish we all did this with more regularity, even more than when we point out how we or others can improve.

There is a much bigger reason to be motivated to do this other than your own confidence. It is to increase your own self-awareness, but more importantly, to be able to lift the confidence of others. The way we hear and understand how others communicate positive information about us helps build our knowledge.

Other people's perspectives increase our own self-awareness more than we know.

If your emotional abilities aren't in hand, if you don't have self-awareness, if you are not able to manage your distressing emotions, if you can't have empathy and have effective relationships, then no matter how smart you are, you are not going to get very far.
—Daniel Goleman

Increased Self-Awareness

On a flight home from Colorado, I read wise words from Tasha Eurich. I was amazed to learn that she found that 95 percent of us believe we are self-aware, when the reality is closer to only 10–15 percent of people are fully self-aware.[55]

Wow. How un-self-aware was I? I wondered. I've made self-awareness my work for a while now, and I help clients do the same.

Was I missing the mark? I pondered.

Eurich measured self-awareness with self-report surveys of individuals and then included reports by those who knew the individuals. When the individuals who took the report realized how off the mark they were, they immediately became more curious about other people's perspectives to increase their ability to identify their own self-awareness more accurately. Eurich states that when you decide there is more to learn about yourself, you become more open to feedback.[56]

> If your emotional abilities aren't in hand, if you don't have self-awareness, if you are not able to manage your distressing emotions, if you can't have empathy and have effective relationships, then no matter how smart you are, you are not going to get very far.
> —Daniel Goleman

Another positive for seeking more accurate information about yourself was revealed in her study of people who made dramatic strides in becoming more self-aware. Those who accepted the challenge to become more self-aware became more selective in their choice of people to ask for feedback.

(I mentally started my list anew at this point. Who had I asked, and who was still left?)

They purposefully chose people they believed had their best interests at heart and would tell the truth, even if the truth was hard. Consequently, they trusted the information and grew in their self-awareness. They also made a concerted effort to not take negative information personally. They gave themselves time to process the data, which helped them understand how to use the information. This is a good point to keep in mind as you start to ponder how to handle insights that come your way using this new framework.

This is when I relaxed. My ASK Framework had served me well. I had been gaining great insights and some hard truths that I had been able to unpack and grow in my own self-awareness. Learning is a forever process, and as I gain wisdom, life lessons, and experience, I hope learning about myself and how I am perceived by others never stops.

The Added Benefit of Asking—Learning!

I called a fellow coach recently. "Have a minute?"

"Sure!" he answered happily.

"The last time we met for our coaches' coffee, I was a fellow presenter. What one thing do you feel I contributed to the group?"

"Wow, Carole. Your participation was a real learning point for a lot of us. You were vulnerable, and when your openness even surprised you, we were right in that moment with you." He paused. "You helped us witness a coaching moment of what vulnerability looked like," he added.

I sat with the phone in my hand.

"Carole, you still there?" he asked softly.

"Yes, I'm sorry. I got lost in thought as I was recalling that moment. I had no idea that was helpful. Actually, I remember that moment differently—I was slightly mortified for getting teary eyed when I shared."

"Carole, that's the point—you were unexpectedly vulnerable, and it allowed us all to see that it was OK to lose our cool sometimes."

After I thanked him, we hung up. I would have never looked at that moment with a positive spin until he offered his perspective.

> Live as if you were to die tomorrow. Learn as if you were to live forever.
> —Mahatma Gandhi

The next time we met, he asked how I was doing with that memory, and I smiled. "Better—thanks to you."

"Good," he replied. "I'm excited to see where these new insights take you, and I know that I can refer people to you who need your experience too."

Self-awareness gives you the capacity to learn from your mistakes as well as your successes. It enables you to keep growing.
—Lawrence Bossidy

Self-awareness gives you the capacity to learn from your mistakes as well as your successes. It enables you to keep growing.
—Lawrence Bossidy

Chapter 12 Questions

1. In this recap, is there anything new that has come up that you are curious to learn about yourself?
2. If you were to learn one new great thing about yourself, how would that shape what you do in your work or personal life in the next ninety days?

What's Next!

S tarting a conversation with context, one thing, and an example can be easy once you get the hang of it. Then the challenge comes. "What next?" and "Where does the conversation go from here?"

Avoiding Why

When I used to call my son at college, I thought I was engaging in quality conversation when I would ask him "why" questions. I was bolstered by questioning concepts like the Five Whys, which originated in Japan and are credited to the founder of Toyota, Sakichi Toyoda.[57] This method was designed to help people get to the root of manufacturing issues but became useful in the start-up world for getting to a point where innovation serves a purpose.[58] This type of questioning focuses the subject to be thoroughly unpacked.

My approach with my son, however, wasn't as focused.

"So tell me why you like the fast food options instead of the foot court we've already paid for?"

"Why do you like your roommate?"

"Why is that class more entertaining than the other class?"

I didn't know why these types of questions would stop the conversation rather than facilitate a better one. I never knew I was making my son defensive until I read Chris Voss's book *Never Split the Difference: Negotiating as if Your Life Depended on It*. Voss's insights helped me see how my approach to conversation irritated my son.

As a "why" child, I grew up asking the why questions people often try to avoid. Not because they don't appreciate the why curiosity of a child—it's the constant asking of the same question all the time that exhausts most. By continuing this practice growing up and never knowing that I was putting people off, I did know that starting meaningful conversations was challenging for me. I just didn't know when to stop the whys and change to better questions that moved the conversation forward.

As a coach now, asking questions is the gateway to helping people think differently, and while I use a variety of insightful questioning styles, my inner child would still want to ask why. Bridging the why desire with what worked professionally was a challenge for me personally.

Voss's insights helped me gain valuable insights into how to move past that challenge.

A hostage negotiator in his professional life, Voss applied many of the tips and techniques he used to successfully end hostage situations, with little injury to either party, effectively in less urgent but frequently tense everyday scenarios.

His book confirms a fascinating perspective for me. When the other party feels heard, you glean the information you need to reveal the next step or end the conversation.

The tips he reveals to improve our everyday negotiations of ordinary circumstances in life—professional and personal—is to not ask "why."[59] Even as I type this, it's still a hard concept for me. Not because I don't understand what he says, but because "why" is an important part of my problem-solving strategy.

As a strategic thinker, defined by Gallup,[60] I start with the why before moving on to understand the who, what, and how. My strategic-thinking leadership style is how I problem solve and until now has been driven by the why of any situation, such as:

"Why are we experiencing this?"

"Why does this topic of conversation matter?" or

"Why is this problem needing to be solved now?"

When I read that Voss believes that asking why puts others on the defensive, I paused. I had never imagined that my problem-solving method caused anyone to go on the defensive. Just as a mirror shows what an object may look like from another perspective, I needed to hear this viewpoint.

I recalled when other people had asked me why. And there it was. I felt defensive, even if it was temporary. Voss says that to get around the big why questions, we need to ask what and how questions.[61]

The problem with defensive communication is that it prevents forward momentum and resolution.

As I thought more about the impact that defensiveness has on effective communication, I recalled a Jack R. Gibb article I had read in the *Journal of Communication*. Originally written in 1961, this article was recirculated in 2007 because it is relevant, and it is important to remember his discovery.

Gibb offered that communication is a people process that relies on a language process and that it is more productive to reduce the degree of defensive communication to improve our interpersonal relationships.[62]

This was a eureka moment for me!

Voss then brought this home for me by showing how changing the way he communicated changed the dynamics within the negotiation/abductor relationships. He understood the risk of creating defensiveness within a hostage situation because lives were—literally—at stake.[63] He now trains other negotiators to communicate the same way.

However, even with this research, I was still confused. How can simply asking why cause another to feel they must defend their answer? Gibbs believes that when someone asks why, the question causes them to spend unnecessary energy and attention on the question and not on the solution. There it was—deflecting focus to the wrong thing.[64]

Now I understood why my own family would say I can come across as a "grill" sergeant. When I was stuck on asking why, my intention was only to get more information, not make people feel attacked. Others didn't receive it that way. I know this showed up at work too.

I recall an abnormally tense exchange with a fellow contractor early in my sales career. I was on a fact-finding mission about a product, and I used my old technique of asking why questions, thinking this was a helpful way to get to more information. Finally, the other contractor turned to me and asked, "Why in the world do you keep asking why!" She was frustrated.

I was a little stunned and taken aback, and—you guessed— feeling defensive.

"I'm just not understanding the purpose behind this product, and I'm needing to grasp that more to communicate its value to the client, that's all," I said.

"I didn't make this product. We just sell it. You can dream up whatever purpose you feel will help the client buy it." And she huffed off.

I realize now that my questioning forced her to recognize she didn't know the answers, and that frustrated us both. We both jumped on the defensive from this line of questioning.

Gibb offered that whenever anyone perceives a threat (real or not), they become defensive and spend extraordinary amounts of energy thinking beyond the question. They start to worry about how they are perceived by you and others and how to avoid further defensive emotions. It becomes a backward-moving conversation, defending themselves.[65]

This helped me understand why people often become defensive when given negative information or asked "why" instead of "what" and "how" questions. Defensive behavior is exhausting and may also be why so many people do not enjoy receiving performance reviews or feedback, specifically when the information given is backward focused. People who offer feedback tend to justify the information, thinking it could be useful moving forward, but few understand how to give it in an appealing or helpful way.

What does this have to do with collecting information about what you do right?

It has more to do with keeping the conversation going.

After someone gets comfortable with the initial framework of "context, one thing, and example" as a conversation starter, I often get the "now what" look from a client while we are role playing. It feels difficult to get comfortable with this new way of gathering positive information, because it's new. It's even newer still to know where to go from there. Here's what I recommend people get comfortable with: repeating the context, one thing, and example—and then learn how to use what and how questions.

Now I can hear you say, "But the brain handles only one thing at a time."

Hear me out. When you repeat the cycle, you're never asking the same question. Rather, you go a little deeper on the same one topic.

This depth helps us fully comprehend the first information offered. It's designed to enhance, not confuse.

I sat down with Cindy, a fellow coach I partnered with on a recent project.

Context: "Cindy, can you share with me a few thoughts on the workshop we just completed?" I asked.

"Sure. What are you curious about?"

One thing: "What do you feel was my greatest contribution to the overall workshop project?"

"Hmm, interesting ask. I would say your greatest contribution was how well you communicated with the client every time we needed more information or there was a change. You have a way of connecting that I don't have—nor do I have the patience. I relied on you a *lot* for that."

Example: "You're kind on that front—they were tough clients. Can you share with me an example of when you saw me do that? I'm not sure I see myself the same way you do."

"Sure! Remember the deadline change that occurred due to a change in content for the workshops? When you sat down with their team, you laid out everything so well for them that they immediately saw the ramifications their new changes had caused—without them even putting up a fight. The new deadline was worked out smoothly, and everyone left happy. You have a gift for reading how the client receives information so much better than I do," she offered.

What/How: "Wow, thanks. I've never considered the way I connect with clients to be a gift"—and here's where I used to ask, "Why do you think that is?" Instead I now ask, "How could we capitalize on the way you and I work with our clients to drive more business?" or "What do you feel would be a great way to market both of our gifts?"

Take time to have conversations with others using what and how questions whenever you'd rather ask why. Use the urge to ask why as a trigger to ask what and how questions instead. It will make the brain work a little differently, and the conversation will move forward more beautifully.

Mastering the Method

Learning to use context, one thing, and example is a big step. Understanding how to continue the conversation with what and how choices allows you flexibility and tools to unpack what you need to understand and explore every aspect of the topic of focus.

Repeating context, one thing, and example, then adding what and how (instead of why) is the master's level to keep your audience open and conversational instead of defensive.

Wash, Rinse, Repeat

Keep in mind, asking questions takes more effort than merely continuing to talk. Remember that you are on a fact-finding hunt, and this interaction is just as valuable to the other person as it is to you.

A good conversation includes a volley of interesting questions and stories, with each person gaining value. The method of context, one thing, and example can be your first step in becoming a valued conversationalist. Even though your initial intent is to gain information about yourself, you now can turn this around to ask about other things. This can lead to an exchange of useful information.

Personal example to a support staff member at work:

Context: "I want to give you something that will make you feel appreciated when you do great work."
One thing: "What type of gift has made you smile in the past?"
Example: "Can you share when you have received a gift like that?"
"Wow, that's a great story! I would love to repeat that experience for you."
What question: "What types of gifts are meaningful to you now?"
How question: "How do you prefer to receive gifts? In private or in front of the givers?"

You can continue this loop with context, one thing, and example or what and how questions interspersed with answers. At the end, you not only have a great sense of what the person would like as a gift but also how they describe a meaningful gift. Do go into the conversation knowing the information you want to gain—don't just wing it, or you will get lost in asking the best questions.

Office meeting example (group): (mixed example)

"When we plan our quarterly goals, what one thing do we consistently get right?"

"How do you recognize that?"

or

"What types of results does your team strive for?"

"How does your team rally together to attain those results?"

"When we get to celebrate their success, what resonates with your team the most?"

"Can you give me an example of how this helps everyone on your team?"

Office example (individual):

"When we all travel for work and it's my turn to do the planning, what is one thing I can do that helps you the most? Can you give me an example of how that helps you?"

"What do you recommend to others in charge of travel plans?"

"What one thing might we never change when planning our travel?"

Remember Sean from chapter 1? This may have been a better conversation for him to step into:

"You have identified an area I excel in, yet you scored my success as only four out of five. What is the most important aspect of this element that you feel I do extremely well?"

"Can you give me an example of a recent time when you recognized that?"

"I'd like to improve enough to score a five. What is the most important thing I can do to achieve that?"

"How do you see me incorporating that into my regular responsibilities?"

"If I were to do that, what support would I look for from the organization?"

The Infinity Circle

You can repeat your context, one thing, and example a few times as long as the focus remains about the one thing. You can also ask what and how questions so you can keep a positive conversation going. The only hard and fast rule is to keep it about the one thing.

We've talked a lot about starting, so now we'll discuss questions. Let's look at an example of working through this cycle several times, incorporating what and how questions to summarize—this is just an example: (Note: Don't deviate from the one topic.)

"Hi, Steve. I'm interested in understanding how to maintain positive performance on our team."

"What is the one thing you feel we currently do that positively affects our current performance?"

"Wow, that's great to hear. Can you give me an example of how you recognize when we are on the right track?"

"What metrics would I pay attention to that support maintaining performance success?"

"Can you share with me how you've kept track of those metrics before?"

Once your questions are answered, end the conversation. Let your brain play with the information you have, and don't get lost on other topics. Getting sidetracked will serve no one well.

Good Conversations Are a Fun Dance

It is a dance between questions and answers, which is how a good conversation can take place. It also provides valuable insight and information you need while making the other person feel valued.

This type of conversation has value and an expiration point. All conversations do. We can't sit around and talk all day if anything is to get done at work. The end of a conversation sets the stage for the next one, so we want to make sure it is a productive experience.

Even a Fun Dance Must End

When we eat a chocolate chip cookie fresh from the oven, we usually want more. Yet reaching for cookie after cookie eventually turns things quite uncomfortable, especially around the waistline. Suddenly, the "ending" of the experience becomes more memorable than its positive beginning.

As we said earlier, our brains simply cannot process a lot of information at one time. Knowing how and when to end the conversation before it becomes "too much" is key to using this technique well.

Consider a great flight to your favorite destination. The flight has been smooth and comfortable, and you got a roomy seat (a girl can dream!). You envision a soft landing, and you're already picturing yourself in your new location.

Then you come in for the landing, and the brakes go out. All hell breaks loose. Skidding down the runway too fast, the plane finally stops. Suddenly your great meal and roomy seat don't seem so great anymore. All you want to do is get off that plane. Some passengers are so traumatized they may never fly again, especially not with that airline.

The same can be said for a conversation. The importance of ending a good conversation with a soft landing is often overlooked. It can be the difference between a productive talk in the future and a shut door that the other person won't reopen. Ending a conversation is just as important as starting it.

Typically, we close conversations with clichéd, comfortable jargon:

"Great! I look forward to talking with you again later."

"I'll let you know how it goes."

"I'll get back to you when you've had more time to think about the question."

Let's take this to a more useful level. Here's an example:

• "Steve, thanks for sharing your thoughts.

- When we started this conversation, I was curious about our team performance,
- and you've offered some great insights.
- Could we follow up in two weeks to share a little more?"

    or

- "Thank you for taking the time to share your thoughts.
- You've given me some great answers about our team performance.
- And you've given me a great example to help me see it from your perspective.
- Can I come to you in the future to ask your input again, perhaps after Tuesday's team meeting? Thanks!"

The goal is to convey your appreciation and to show Steve that you value his input. You've also brought closure, letting him know the conversation was valuable for now and possibly in the future as well. You can check the box for productivity, and everyone can move on with their day.

This method is like landing a plane on a smooth runway: no wind, perfect tires, and a gliding descent. You can rush it or prolong it. Either way, it's a tight, kind, friendly, and appreciative way to convey how much you enjoyed hearing what they had to say and to keep the door open for the future.

> Communicate to the other person as you would want him to communicate to you if your positions were reversed.
> —Aaron Goldman

Communicate to the other person as you would want him to communicate to you if your positions were reversed.
—Aaron Goldman

Chapter 13 Questions

1. What is one scenario you can see improving by using the ASK Framework in a wash, rinse, repeat cycle?
2. Is there one thing holding you back from getting started? Write it down and consider how to address that obstacle.

Bringing It Home

When work experiences are great, we bring home the good vibes.

When work experiences are not great, we bring that home too.

It's hard to disconnect the work portion of our day from the family and friend portion of our day.

On a great day, you feel happy when you return home. Suddenly you have the energy to help with homework, play catch in the backyard, or accomplish chores. Your family is thrilled with your good mood. They know it probably came from a good day at work. Whether or not they are interested in the details, they care that it made their time with you more pleasant.

Contrast that with the results of a bad day. You come home brooding and tired, with no energy to help with anything. Instead, you just want to sulk somewhere by yourself or escape in front of the television. Maybe a movie will keep your mind off whatever made you mad or sad at work. Bad days drive people to retreat internally and shut out the very people who could encourage them.

When You Share with Those Who Matter Most

"Jimmy! Where are you?" Frank hollered out with excitement.

"What, Dad? Is everything OK?" Jimmy came running around the corner.

"You have *got* to hear this!"

Frank excitedly shared how he stepped into his boss's office and asked what his boss felt he contributed to the project they were working on. Frank was so surprised to hear what his boss thought that he couldn't wait to share it with Jimmy.

"Jimmy, all that math I get to help you with really sharpened my own skills at work. The last meeting, I was able to catch a math glitch that could have really caused a lot of delays in the prototype we were working on," Frank said. "My boss told me I saved them almost a million dollars with that math catch, and he was so thankful I was a part of that team! And the best part, Jimmy, I have you to thank for reminding me how important math is all the time."

Yes, tell your family and friends what others share with you and what it means to you. Share how you feel and what you think about that information. Include them in future brainstorming of what you want to learn about yourself and who to ask. Consider the interesting conversation over the dinner table as others realize they can use this method too.

"Hi, Mom! How was work?" Sarah greeted her mother as she came in.

"Hi, Sarah. It was really great today. You want to know why?" Beth's eyes twinkled. "My boss told me that my networking helped land the company a new contract today, and we are celebrating tonight!" Beth glowed.

"What's networking?" Sarah asked.

As Beth explained networking to Sarah, she realized how often she didn't share the fundamentals of work to Sarah either. Sarah had no idea what she did. From that night on, Beth came home with new stories about what she did so that Sarah could learn more.

> I think one day you'll find that you're the hero you've been looking for.
> —Jimmy Stewart

Remember, when you share positive things that happen at work, your family is learning from you.

Set the Example

Sharing information about what you do right sets an example. You are sharing with them a part of you in a way that helps them see your skills as useful, successful, and potentially duplicatable. When you tell them how others see you at work, your family gets to share and support your success. When they know how others view your success, they have more confidence in your ability to be successful, for yourself and for the family.

This often strengthens your support at home, so when things get tough at work and you need to work late, they may make sacrifices, cheer you on, and be more patient than before.

Share What Your Family Does

Imagine taking this a step further and sharing the things your family members do well with them too.

- **Context:** "Whenever you help set the table for dinner,
- **One thing:** you always make sure everyone has all their silverware and napkins."
- **Example:** "When you set the table, you make sitting down to eat much easier. Thank you!"

Sports example:

- **Context:** "This week when I watched you play volleyball,
- **One thing:** I noticed that you cheer on your teammates."
- **Example:** "This tells your team that you are paying attention to them and have their back. It's a great thing to do, and I'm sure they appreciate it."

What would this positive conversation look like in *your* house? How would it make the members of your household feel? Telling them about the things they do well, that you notice, will help them understand what they contribute to the family and potentially the world.

When you get to find what you do to make a positive difference at work, use the same concept to support your own family at home. They will start to pay attention to what you see and what you tell them. This positive approach is far more effective than always telling them what they are doing wrong or need to improve.

And remember, it's your family, so they're already emotionally connected to you. You can have great impact on their growth if you use a positive approach.

> Rational thoughts never drive people's creativity the way emotions do.
> —Neil deGrasse Tyson

Concentrating on what is going right will get more of their positive attention. The neuroscience behind this is growing. Just think what a gift this would be for your kids, extended family, and friends. Concentrating on what the people around you do right can revitalize your relationships with them.

Let's look at specific age groups.

Your Kids

Babies. Such a cool time if you stop to realize how amazingly babies grow. I didn't when I had mine, which may be why I am so excited to be a grandmother. It's like a great do-over while I'm also giving my own kids a break from parenting.

Babies

Babies build brain cells faster than you can count. Watch them open and close a box over and over, and you're watching a continual growth process. It's fascinating!

Providing adequate support and space for this activity builds their thinking skills and confidence. It also helps neurotransmitters to build, connect, and work as they could. I recently watched my own young grandson discover that small polished rocks will roll around a bathtub and go around the corners and keep going. It was loud, he laughed, and he kept doing it until he was tired of it.

I experimented with the concept of letting him know what he was doing right. When he put the rocks back, we celebrated.

When he laughed, we hugged. When he thought about throwing the rocks out of the tub, we stopped and repeated what worked well before: rolling, laughing, putting them back. Using affection and enjoyment, I reinforced the behavior I needed from him. This is what doctors refer to as "positive priming."

We prime our brains all the time. We tell babies no to protect them from hurting themselves. Be careful not to tell them no just for the sake of it. Be selective in its use. Remember that you are making the most impact on what they learn, how they learn it, and how they practice using their curiosity with positive results. Each child is unique with their own set of strengths. This is a parent's or grandparent's golden moment: watching how they take in information, gaining their trust, learning what makes them laugh and what they concentrate on.

Get to know your kid as they take in the world; watch and observe, and you will see how each is unique, powerful, and smart. When you do, they trust that you care and want to be with them too. Mutual trust builds a great foundation for learning.

Kids

The help you give them when they're babies will have lasting effects on them as they grow up. If we tell kids what they do right more often than we tell them what they do wrong, we build their confidence faster than desert flowers bloom after a rain.

Every time you tell a kid what they are doing right, it takes root. When you provide an example, you give them a picture of what they can keep doing. These mental snapshots remind them of how they accomplished it, reinforcing the behaviors associated with it, and they also remember how the comfort of positive emotions felt.

This is helpful, as they link rewards to expectations. Hearing what they do right is the reward, the example is what you expect of them in the future, and the context shows them exactly when it applies. This helps them repeat positive habits instead of guessing.

In contrast, when you just tell a kid they've done something wrong, they often simply guess what to do next. However, if you provide context, explain what they did wrong, and give an example of what you saw them do and what you wish they'd done, this helps them understand your perspective. And when that happens, they'll often open up and tell you more, allowing you to better understand where they are in their own learning functions of right and wrong. Kids need to learn from your perspective—and share theirs—so they can figure out what works and doesn't work. Even if they don't agree, they'll know how you see things.

"Johnny, when you were playing with your little sister, what were you expecting to happen when you hit her hand like that?"

"I don't know," Johnny said sheepishly.

"What was she doing that made you so mad, you felt you needed to do that?"

"She kept taking my favorite toy and running away—I just wanted to play with it, and she kept taking it!" Johnny's eye's flashed with frustration.

"OK, I get it. That must have been frustrating. Do you think she wanted to play with you and that's how she was trying to do that?"

Johnny paused. "Maybe."

"Tell you what. I get it that she can frustrate you. I think she really admires you and wants your attention. If I can keep her playing for a little while with me, what would you like to play with her when you're done here?"

"Oh, I can play blocks with her!" he said helpfully.

"OK, let's set the timer for one hour for you to play here, and I'll keep her busy. You can play with her when the timer goes off. She'll be really excited."

When kids talk, you'll see the world through their eyes. Be patient. Let them explain. When they get stuck, ask questions that help you understand more without making them feel small or stupid. Shutting down conversations with a kid belittles them and teaches them to trust you less.

If they sense you don't want to help them learn or if you don't make them feel respected or accepted, you'll confuse and frustrate them, and they'll pull away. This lays the foundation for them to withhold information from you in the future.

Piquing their curiosity helps.

They will be open, trust more, and communicate their feelings. Teaching them how to think about context, asking for what they've done right, and asking for an example is a huge confidence booster for them.

"Johnny, I just want you to know that I'm glad you shared that you were frustrated. That helps me know you are trying to be the best you. When you share your feelings, it helps me understand how to help faster, and I like to help you feel better any time I can."

When a kid sees a parent think through a problem and then hears the parent praise them for what they did that made a positive impact, the kid feels empowered. They'll feel more confident, and the satisfaction this gives them will overflow into your conversations with them.

> Flying is learning how to throw yourself at the ground and miss.
> —Douglas Adams

Too often we concentrate on always teaching kids what to do better, what to learn next, and how to improve, and we forget to balance it by also teaching them what they don't need to change. Confidence is a precious gift. It gives them resilience and great memories.

Parenting is not easy, yet great communication doesn't have to be hard. Even young kids can benefit from learning to share how they feel. For example, if you ask them about why they need you to help them with their shoes every morning, you might get this (kid to parent example):

- **Context:** "Every day when we hurry out the door for school,
- **One thing:** you always help me put on my shoes."
- **Example:** "When you do this, I know you won't leave without me, and that feels good."

Learn to recognize the times when your child needs to know the good things they do. As parents, we often forget to balance the good with the need to improve, teach, change, or parent our kids.

Teenagers

Studies have shown that girls start to second-guess themselves as soon as their bodies begin to change.[66] Boys do as well; they simply seem to change later than girls.[67] In my experience, if teens can't control their growth, they try to figure out what they can control.

Girls will lash out, becoming emotional and frustrated by the smallest changes at school and home. Boys become either more talkative or withdrawn. They spend more time alone or with friends rather than with parents. Be kind; be patient; be there for them when they need to talk or vent. This stage will pass. Yet this is the *best* time to remind them what you see them doing well. Not in an oppressive "I expect this from you always" manner—they do *not* need any more pressure than society already places on them. Listen with the intention that you care about what they think because they matter.

Do resist the urge to be their friend instead of their parent. At this stage, teach them how to look at context and how it helps them control the topic of conversation.

Let's pick their most recent report card as the topic. Let's assume that they make average grades and there may be a few lower-than-expected grades. Ask them what they feel they do well and don't think they need to change. Celebrate the good in every way possible *before* addressing anything unexpected.

This lessens the stress and allows them to focus on what is working for them. It frees up their brain so they can start to embrace what it would feel like if the whole report card was the way they wanted it to be, and it builds their confidence in what they are currently doing well. You can also teach them to use this method to ask their teacher for examples of what they are doing that does not need to change. This way, they'll understand how the teacher views their work.

I wish I had known to do this when my kids were teenagers. I am not proud to say I did the opposite. Yelling at them for not making top grades. Trying to instill in them that they are better than average. Never asking them the questions that count so that they felt heard. I remember one such conversation with my son.

"I see that your grade in math is really dipping," I started.

"The teacher is so tough, Mom, and I'm just struggling with this class," my son countered.

"Then you need to spend more time studying" was my logical reply.

"Mom, maybe I'm just not that good in this level of math. Maybe I'm just meant to be average in this class."

"Absolutely not! I do not raise you kids to settle for being average. You are too smart to give up!" I retorted, as if these statements would light a fire for his motivation.

"What's wrong with being average?!" my son angrily replied.

I stopped in my tracks. I was stunned he felt so angry. I don't remember the way I continued, but it wasn't healthy, and I still wasn't asking him any questions about the way he thought, felt, or wanted to continue to succeed in this subject. But I will never forget his frustration with my goals over his that day.

Perhaps that is why I know this works, as I started using this technique to get to know my children as soon as I learned it. And I use it today to get to know my new grandchildren as they grow and learn to talk. Use the ASK formula in reverse to share what you love about your kids. Teach it to them to use at school and when they start to work. This will satisfy their desire for feedback and allow them to go after the information that counts when they need it.

By teaching this formula, your teens will gain the ability to start meaningful conversations that provide important details. You will help your teen develop the skills of critical thinking and of approaching people in authority. They will also learn the concepts of context and examples. The more comfortable they become in gathering data about what they do right, the more confidence they gain in collaborating with authority figures as they mature.

> Optimism is a happiness magnet. If you stay positive, good things and good people will be drawn to you.
> —Mary Lou Retton

College-Age Young Adults

Young adults fascinate me. They are of age to vote, enlist in the armed services, and go to college. Yet science has revealed that a young man's body is still growing until age twenty-five, and both genders struggle with emotional intelligence as they embrace the new prospects of becoming full-fledged adults.

When they are away at college or working on their own and come home to visit, they want some of the old, yet they want you to be curious and open about their new life. You are home base to them. They need some things to stay the same so they can reflect, review, and debate what they want to change or celebrate in themselves. Their full-time job is to learn and perform on a larger scale, and it does amazing things to their viewpoint and perspective. Often they want to explore this with you too. Be open. Don't shut them down or make them feel less-than because of their viewpoints. Instead, be curious and ask questions. You can use the "one thing" here in unique ways.

- **Context:** "In all your classes this semester,
- **One thing:** what was the most unique thing you've learned?"
- **Example:** "Give me an example of how that changed your perspectives."

By showing interest and asking questions like this, you make them feel valued. Your specific context of choice allows them to be clear about the topic. Your question forces them to choose one thing rather than talking about everything. When you ask for an example, the conversation will become rich. This is when you'll hear their new viewpoint on the world, see how they've changed, or learn how their perspectives have shifted. This also gives you a unique opportunity to see where they've grown since leaving high school.

Offer to teach them this concept of asking questions, yet sell it in a useful way for them in an academic setting or in a work setting. Understanding how the instructor or manager sees the world and sees your young adult's work can mean the difference between average and excellence.

For college kids, if their first job offer is potentially based on GPA rankings, this can be a big deal. Offer to give them a tip that has helped you in your career. Only offer if they're interested. They'll ask you to tell them. They might not be interested, or they may act as if you're too old to tell them anything useful. If so, then simply let them know that, if they want the information later, they can ask for it. They will probably either ask right then or come back soon. Your words will stay in their head. Respect the space they need to get over their own young egos.

Don't make your ego more important than theirs.

Your Spouse

When you want to dive into a fun conversation with the person you think you know best, try this with your spouse. We all change daily, due to our work and personal interactions outside the home. But we often don't have time to share those changes and interactions with our family or spouse. This can cause people to drift apart if we don't recognize it and make changes. The "one thing" conversation is a great place to start.

- **Context:** "We've been crazy busy. I'd love to stay connected with what's going on with you."
- **One thing:** "What's been the best thing that happened to you this week?"
- **Example:** "How did that happen, and how did it make you feel?"

Or:

- **Context:** "I don't want us to forget to connect."
- **One thing:** "What's one thing I can do this week to remind you that I love you?"
- **Example:** "Can you provide me an example of how you need to see that?"

How joyful and prosperous you will be! Your wife will be like a fruitful grapevine, flourishing within your home. Your children will be like vigorous young olive trees as they sit around your table.

Psalm 128:2–3

Chapter 14 Questions

1. What is an activity that your child or spouse does every day that you would like to explore with them? It can be a hobby, a job, or even an annoying habit.
2. Using the ASK steps, write a question that leads to gaining a greater understanding and appreciation for this regular habit or activity of theirs.

Teach Someone Else

Those who know, do. Those that understand, teach.
—Aristotle

Teaching someone else reveals how much we know. You get to choose whom to teach. It could be your direct reports, colleagues, staff, kids, grandkids, family members, or friends. Start with people who come to you for advice and those at work who look to you for guidance and support. If you have an interest in their success, they are a candidate.

Teaching someone how to find out what they do right is a gift that will keep on giving for their entire career and life. Let them know that this technique will allow them to gain the feedback they desire, regardless of where they are—work or someplace else. Teach this to them by having them shape the context, ask what they do that makes a positive impact, and ask for an example.

Since you know them, you can easily give them insight. Offering to teach them allows them to hear what they do well from your perspective. This is meaningful and allows them to appreciate what you have to offer, making the experience positive from every angle.

Once you've worked one on one, challenge them to ask one other person to practice with. Then have them come back and tell you what they learned. When they do, ask how they feel about this information, what it makes them think about, and how they plan to stay productive with this new information.

Failing and messing up is fine. Just have them practice again. This provides you both with great information to build around as they look to improve in new areas after they've learned what they don't need to change. In the last chapter, we talked about the impact this can have on your family. What about important adults in your life?

Consider your friends, neighbors, siblings, parents, cousins, church members, community sports teams, volunteer members, and so on. These adults may see you far differently than you realize. Teaching this to others not only helps you both have great conversations but also helps you learn from each other about what you do right from another's perspective.

Adult example: brother

- **Context:** "Brian, you were always there for me at school."
- **One thing:** "What is the one thing I do that lets you know I'm there for you too?"
- **Example:** "Can you give me an example of a time when I've done that?"

A good teacher must be able to put himself in the place of those who find learning hard. —Eliphas Levi

Regardless of Brian's answer, this is a great place for a conversation to happen. If Brian says he doesn't recognize your desire to be there for him, you can have a conversation about that and offer your perspective. Often, we don't always recognize another's intent until we are told. This becomes something you can now offer him, discuss how he recognizes support, and talk about how he would identify the change now that he knows your intent.

If someone wants to know why you started asking these questions, this provides an opportunity to tell them the advantages of finding out what's going right before looking for ways to improve. This concept often intrigues people, and they'll want to learn how it works. Give the information and challenge them to use it with one person they trust to have something positive to offer. Then challenge them to use this with one person at work and let you know what they find out. This type of fun challenge creates great conversations later.

Watching how you interact, others will learn quickly. Hearing what you've found out about yourself provides results and meaning. Practicing it with people you trust allows you to try the method without fearing failure and then evaluate your experience. You, as an adult, learn through experiences and needs.

I encourage you to allow others to see you do it first, hear how you have benefited, and then try it out for themselves. This approach is supported by Rutgers University research. This research reveals that adults need to be involved in planning their instruction and evaluating their results.[68] Learning takes place best in an environment in which mistakes are safe, expected, and seen as a basis for continued learning. For the most part, adults have little time to learn new content for its own sake. Instead, they are interested in approaching tasks related to their occupation. To thrive in most learning opportunities, they need to understand how each lesson fits into their goals.

Children are taught to view instructors as authority figures who challenge their own knowledge. Adults expect that even the most credentialed expert will be their partner in learning.

The Fun of It

When you learn how to use and teach this tool, it becomes more than just a fun, handy tool to own and share. It soon develops into a superpower all its own that you can give someone else.

The first time I tried this, I had little faith that the conversation would even allow me to get to the example. I was wrong. I provided the context as a preface to the conversation and asked for the one thing they felt I did right and not to change. Then I faced the option of either chatting about the one thing or asking for the example.

> The beautiful thing about learning is nobody can take it away from you.
> —B. B. King

I struggled with this; I suspect you will too. It's an odd new habit to form. When I chose to ask for the example, my coworker surprised me. The example she gave was something I had no idea she even paid attention to. This powerful tool gives such pleasant and unexpected results that I purposefully use it for collecting examples that I can leverage with work and, in addition, for the fun of connecting with friends and family.

What It Does for You

Here are a few bonus ideas to try. Often when I ask someone to tell me something I do right and to give an example, I don't appreciate it until later when I have time to think about it. This gift provides me with unique insights, which I ruminate on in the days following the conversation. I love discovering how other people view me and how they view the world differently. It's a little like escaping into a book and seeing a whole world that's different than your own.

When I ask people how it felt when I asked them these questions, they say it felt new, like a completely different way to share but on a deeper level they hadn't experienced before. They marvel at the questions' simplicity and the inspiration they felt when thinking about their answers. Telling me about their memories and emotions made them feel good because they knew it allowed them to share a part of themselves.

Once you replace negative thoughts with positive ones, you start having positive results.
—Willie Nelson

Sharing what people do well feels good. If you knew who made the best pizza in the world, you'd want to tell others about it so everyone could experience it. If you had the best news in the world, you'd want to share it. If you know what someone else does well, sharing it with them is a gift. The emotions that come from sharing and explaining what is going right are the ingredients for a Hallmark movie. Why wouldn't you share it? Why wouldn't you do it?

The most positive thing we can do in this world is to positively build up another. When we discover the things we do that positively impact others, these are the things we don't need to change. When we find out what to treasure about ourselves, we get to breathe a little easier, celebrate our unique talents, share them with the world, and lean into who we are meant to be.

So encourage each other and build each other up, just as you are already doing.
1 Thessalonians 5:11

Once you replace negative thoughts with positive ones, you start having positive results.
—Willie Nelson

Chapter 15

1. Who is one person you would love to help learn this ASK method?
2. How do you see this ASK Framework being a benefit to this person's satisfaction and growth?
3. When will you begin modeling this method so they can see the value?

Notes

Introduction

1. Jack Canfield and Mark Victor Hansen, *The Aladdin Factor: How to Ask for What You Want—and Get It* (NY: Penguin, 1995).

2. Douglas Stone and Sheila Heen, *Thanks for the Feedback: The Science and Art of Receiving Feedback Well* (New York: Penguin Books) 2014, 3.

3. Tania, Katan, "4 Ways to Quiet Imposter Syndrome and Start Believing in Yourself," in *Idea.Ted.Com*, May 21, 2019, ideas.ted.com/4-ways-to-quiet-imposter-syndrome-and-start-believing-in-yourself/.

4. Christina Loffredo, "Combating Invisibility: Seeing the Unseen in a Virtual Workforce," *CCI Consulting*, July 8, 2020, www.cciconsulting.com/combating-invisibility/.

Chapter 2

5. Jon D. Holtzman, "Food and Memory," *Annual Review of Anthropology*, vol. 35, no. 1, (2006): 361–378, doi/10.1146/annurev.anthro.35.081705.123220.

6. Dolores M. Merino and Jesús Privado, "Does Employee Recognition Affect Positive Psychological Functioning and Well-Being?" *The Spanish Journal of Psychology*, vol. 18 (2015): E64., doi:10.1017/sjp.2015.67.

7. "How to Build Productivity through Reward & Recognition," *Bamboo HR*, July 8, 2020, www.bamboohr.com/webinars/productivity-reward-recognition/.

8. Selena Rezvani and Kelly Monahan, PhD, "The Millennial Mindset: Work Styles and Aspirations of Millennials," *Deloitte*, 2017, www2.deloitte.com/content/dam/Deloitte/us/Documents/process-and-operations/us-cons-millennial-mindset.pdf.

9. "Big Demands and High Expectations: The Deloitte Millennial Survey" Deloitte, 2014, https://www2.deloitte.com/content/dam/Deloitte/global/Documents/About-Deloitte/gx-dttl-2014-millennial-survey-report.pdf.

10. Annita Lettink, "No, Millennials Will NOT Be 75% of the Workforce in 2025 (or Ever)!" LinkedIn, 2019, https://www.linkedin.com/pulse/millennials-75-workforce-2025-ever-anita-lettink/.

11. "How to Build Productivity through Reward & Recognition," bamboHR, https://www.bamboohr.com/webinars/productivity-reward-recognition/.

12. Glenn Llopis, "10 Signs Your Employees are Growing Complacent in Their Careers," *Forbes*, July 8, 2013, www.forbes.com/sites/glennllopis/2013/07/08/10-signs-your-employees-are-growing-complacent-in-their-careers/#3993aff5722c

13. "The Importance of Positive Feedback and How to Deliver it to Others," Indeed, April 18, 2019, www.indeed.com/career-advice/career-development/importance-of-positive-feedback.

14. "How to Build Productivity through Reward & Recognition," bamboHR.

15. "Get Looped In on 'Feedback': Its History Is More Than Just Noise," Merriam Webster, www.merriam-webster.com/words-at-play/the-history-of-feedback.

16. A. Walker and J. W. Smither, "A Five Year Study of Upward Feedback: What Managers Do with Their Results Matters," *Personnel Psychology*, vol. 52, no. 2 (1999): 393–423, in *APA PsycNet*, doi/abs/10.1111/j.1744-6570.1999.tb00166.x.

Chapter 3

17. Maika Leibbrandt, "Strengths: Why You Are Even More Special Than 1 in a Million," Gallup, August 28, 2013, www.gallup.com/cliftonstrengths/en/251552/strengths-why-even-more-special-million.aspx.

18. Taken from my notes from a presentation by Sheila Heen (who with author Douglas Stone wrote *Thanks for the Feedback: The Science and Art of Receiving Feedback Well*), speaking at the DC HRM Conference, June 2016.

19. Stefan P. Cantore and David L. Cooperrider, "Positive Psychology and Appreciative Inquiry: The Contribution of the Literature to an Understanding of the Nature and Process of Change in Organizations," in *The Wiley-Blackwell Handbook of the Psychology of Leadership, Change, and Organizational Development* eds. H. S. Leonard, R. Lewis, A. M. Freedman, and J. Passmore, (Wiley Blackwell, 2013): 267–287, https://doi.org/10.1002/9781118326404.ch13.

20. M. M. Gergen, K. J. Barrett, and F. Gergen, "Appreciative Inquiry as Dialogue: Generative and Transformative," *Constructive Discourse and Human Organization*, vol. 1, eds. D. L. and M. Avital (Emerald Group Publishing Limited, 2004), 3–27, in *Emerald Insight*, doi/10.1016/S1475-9152(04)01001-4/full/html.

21. "Why Do We Need Endorphins?" *Healthline*, July 11, 2017, www.healthline.com/health/endorphins#takeaway.

22. B. L Fredrickson, et al, "Open Hearts Build Lives: Positive Emotions, Induced through Loving-Kindness Meditation, Build Consequential Personal Resources," *Journal of Personality and Social Psychology*, vol. 95, no. 5, (200): 1045–1062, in *APA PsycNet*, doi.apa.org/doiLanding?doi=10.1037%2Fa0013262.

23. "Understanding the Stress Response: Chronic Activation of This Survival Mechanism Impairs Health," *Harvard Health Publishing*, July 6, 2020, www.health.harvard.edu/staying-healthy/understanding-the-stress-response.

Chapter 4

24. Todd B, Kashdan, *Curious? Discover the Missing Ingredient to a Fulfilling Life*, reprint (New York: Harper Perennial, 2010), Audible version,

25. Todd B, Kashdan, *Curious? Discover the Missing Ingredient to a Fulfilling Life*, Audible version.

26. Marc Trussler Stuart and Soroka, "Consumer Demand for Cynical and Negative News Frames," *The International Journal of Press and Politics* (March 18, 2014): 360–379.

27. Tom Stafford, "Why Bad News Dominates the Headlines," *BBC Future*, BBC 28, July 2014.

Chapter 5

28. Douglas Stone and Sheila Heen, *Thanks for the Feedback: The Science and Art of Receiving Feedback Well*, 247–258.

29. "The Multitasking Myth: The Science behind 'One Thing at a Time' Holds True," *The One Thing* blog, https://www.the1thing.com/blog/the-one-thing/the-multitasking-myth-the-science-behind-one-thing-at-a-time-holds-true/.

30. The Multitasking Myth: The Science behind 'One Thing at a Time' Holds True," *The One Thing* blog, https://www.the1thing.com/blog/the-one-thing/the-multitasking-myth-the-science-behind-one-thing-at-a-time-holds-true/.

31. Julia Schmidt, et al, "Feedback Interventions for Impaired Self-awareness Following a Brain Injury: A Systematic Review," *Journal of Rehabilitation Medicine*, vol. 43, no. 8 (July 2011): 673–680, in *Ingenta Connect*, doi. org/10.2340/16501977-0846.

32. Peter R. Dickson and Norris Krueger Jr., "How Believing in Ourselves Increases Risk Taking: Perceived Self-Efficacy and Opportunity Recognition," *Decision Sciences*, vol. 24, no.3 (May 1994): 385–400, in *Wiley Online Library*, onlinelibrary.wiley.com/doi/abs/10.1111/j.1540-5915.1994. tb00810.x.

33. Deborah Sole and Daniel G. Wilson, "Storytelling in Organizations: The Power and Traps of Using Stories to Share Knowledge in Organizations," Learning Innovations Laboratory, n.d, 1–12, http://www.providersedge.com/docs/km_articles/Storytelling_in_Organizations.pdf.

34. "Stickiness," *Marketing Terms*, www.marketingterms.com/dictionary/stickiness/.

Chapter 6

35. L. Froman, "Positive Psychology in the Workplace," *Journal of Adult Development*, vol. 17 (2010): 59–69, *Springer*

Link, doi.org/10.1007/s10804-009-9080-0. Also see Stefan P. Cantore and David L. Cooperrider, "Positive Psychology and Appreciative Inquiry: The Contribution of the Literature to an Understanding of the Nature and Process of Change in Organizations," *The Wiley-Blackwell Handbook of the Psychology of Leadership, Change, and Organizational Development*, eds. H. Skipton Leonard, et al (West Sussex, UK: John Wiley & Sons Ltd., 2016).

Chapter 7

36. Mark Tarallo, "Viewpoint: Your First 90 Days as a New Manager," *SHRM*, February 19, 2020, shrm.org/resourcesandtools/hr-topics/organizational-and-employee-development/pages/viewpoint-your-first-90-days-as-a-new-manager.aspx.

37. "Managing the Employee Onboarding and Assimilation Process," SHRM, June 30, 2020, www.shrm.org/resourcesandtools/tools-and samples/toolkits/pages/onboardingandassimilationprocess.aspx.

Chapter 8

38. Jim Asplund, et al, "The Clifton StrengthsFinder 2.0 Technical Report: Development and Validation," *Gallup*, March 2014, www.gallup.com/services/176321/clifton-strengthsfinder-technical-report-development-validation.aspx.

39. A meeting at a local SHRM chapter gathering offered this insight. The topic was diversity and inclusion, how the way we think biases our perceptions. "Diversity and Inclusion: How the Way We Think Biases Our Perceptions," SHRM chapter, Reston, Virginia, 2018.

40. Corinne Post, et al, "Capitalizing on Thought Diversity for Innovation," *Journal of Research-Technology Management*, vol. 52, no. 6 (December 22, 2015): 14–25, in *Taylor and Francis Online*, doi/abs/10.1080/08956308.2009.1165759.

41. Sarah Lewis, "Using Appreciative Inquiry in Sales Team Development," *Industrial and Commercial Training*, vol. 40, no. 4 (June 13, 2008): 175–180, in *Emerald Insight*, doi/10.1108/00197850810876217.

42. Marcial Losada and Emily Heaphy, "The Role of Positivity and Connectivity in the Performance of Business Teams: A Nonlinear Dynamics Model," *American Behavioral Scientist*, vol, 47, no. 6 (February 1, 2004), in *Sage Journals*, doi/10.1177/0002764203260208.

Chapter 9

43. James Clear, *Atomic Habits: An Easy & Proven Way to Build Habits & Break Bad Ones* (NY: Penguin Random House, 2018), 74.

44. James Clear, *Atomic Habits: An Easy & Proven Way to Build Habits & Break Bad Ones*, 70–73.

45. Ryan Holiday, "Here's the Mindset of Elite Athletes," *Thrive Global*, September 18, 2018, medium.com/thrive-global/ heres-the-mindset-of-elite-athletes-53c6ecd5e3a6.

46. "Impact of Physician Fitness and Mindset to Michael Jordan's Sports Greatness," *Sports Mockery*, May 26, 2020, sportsmockery.com/2020/05/impact-of-physical-fitness-and-mindset-to-michael-jordans-sports-greatness/.

47. Vanessa Van Edwards, "Asking for Advice: Why It Can Actually Bring You Closer to Others," *Science of People*, July 16, 2020, www.scienceofpeople.com/asking-advice/.

48. Jon Youshaei, "Ten Ways to Think Like Jeff Bezos," *Forbes*, December 19, 2017, www.forbes.com/sites/jonyoushaei/2017/12/19/10-ways-to-think-like-jeff-bezos/#7f0fff4e64a1.

Chapter 10

49. Bill Durkin, "Positive Questions Create Positive Results," *One Positive Place*, April 15, 2016, www.onepositiveplace.com/single-post/2016/04/15/Positive-Questions-Create-Positive-Results.

50. "Communication: The Importance of Context." *Engaged HR*, August 17, 2016, engagedhr.com/the-importance-of-context/.

Chapter 11

51. "Should," *Oxford English Dictionary*, 2020, www.lexico.com/en/definition/should.

52. Tinus Van de Merwe and Brian Kelly, "Stop Playing the Victim: How to Shift Up and Out of Dependence," *Human Capital Business Solutions*, July 13, 2018, hcbsolutions.com/2018/07/13/the-toxicity-of-dependence/.

53. Lisa C. Gregory, DeAnna Murphy, Steve Jeffs, "6 Critical Things You Must Do to Effectively Lead During These Uncertain Times—You Are Not Powerless," *People Acuity*, April 7, 2020, peopleacuity.com/author/dmurphypeopleacuity-com/.

54. Lisa C. Gregory, DeAnna Murphy, Steve Jeffs, "6 Critical Things You Must Do to Effectively Lead During These Uncertain Times—You Are Not Powerless."

Chapter 12

55. Tasha Eurich, *Insight: The Surprising Truth about How Others See Us, How We See Ourselves, and Why the Answers Matter More Than We Think* (NY: Penguin Random House, 2018, New York), 42.

56. Tasha Eurich, *Insight: The Surprising Truth about How Others See Us, How We See Ourselves, and Why the Answers Matter More Than We Think*, 42.

Chapter 13

57. Taiichi Ohno, *Toyota Production System: Beyond Large-Scale Production* (Boca Raton, FL: Taylor & Francis Group, 1988).

58. Eric Ries, "The Five Whys for Start-Ups," *Harvard Business Review*, April 30, 2010, https://hbr.org/2010/04/the-five-whys-for-startups.

59. Chris Voss, *Never Split the Difference: Negotiating as if Your Life Depended on It* (Harper Audio, 2016), Audible version.

60. "Understanding the Strategic Thinking Domain of CliftonStrengths," *Gallup*, July 16, 2020, www.gallup.com/cliftonstrengths/en/252080/strategic-thinking-domain.aspx.

61. Chris Voss, *Never Split the Difference: Negotiating as if Your Life Depended on It*, Audible version.

62. Jack R. Gibb, "Defensive Communication," *Journal of Communication*, vol. 11, no. 3 (1961): 141–148, in *Wiley Online Library*, doi/abs/10.1111/j.1460-2466.1961.tb00344.x.

63. Chris Voss, *Never Split the Difference: Negotiating as if Your Life Depended on It*, Audible version.

64. Jack R. Gibb, "Defensive Communication."

65. Jack R. Gibb, "Defensive Communication."

Chapter 14

66. "What Makes Teen Depression Different form Adult Depression?," Hunting Beach Christian Counseling, May 30, 2018, https://huntingtonbeachchristiancounseling.com/articles/what-makes-teen-depression-different-from-depression-in-adults/.

67. "Understanding Puberty," reviewed by Steven Dowshen, *Kids Health*, 2015, shorturl.at/kuGHI.

Chapter 15

68. Melinda Malik, "Assessment of a Professional Development Program on Adult Learning Theory," *Libraries and the Academy*, vol. 16, no. 1 (2016): 47–70, at *Project Muse*, muse.jhu.edu/article/609810.

ORDER INFORMATION

CPSIA information can be obtained
at www.ICGtesting.com
Printed in the USA
FSHW020409120122
87553FS

9 781683 148388